WILLIAM CARLOS WILLIA

William Carlos Williams

AN AMERICAN ARTIST

James E. Breslin

New York
OXFORD UNIVERSITY PRESS 1970

Grateful acknowledgment is given to the following publishers for permission to reprint from their publications:

Beacon Press for *I Wanted To Write a Poem* by William Carlos Williams, edited by Edith Heal. Copyright © 1958 by William Carlos Williams.

City Lights Books for *Kora in Hell* by William Carlos Williams. Copyright 1920 and © 1957 by The Four Seas Company, Boston.

New Directions Publishing Corporation for letter to his brother (1908), including poem about Isadora Duncan, copyright © 1970 by Florence H. Williams; *Collected Earlier Poems*, copyright 1938, 1951 by William Carlos Williams; *Paterson*, copyright 1946, 1948, 1949, 1951, © 1958 by William Carlos Williams; *Paterson*, Book VI, copyright © 1963 by Florence H. Williams; *Pictures from Brueghel and Other Poems*, copyright 1954 by William Carlos Williams; *Poems*, all rights reserved; *In the American Grain*, copyright 1925 by James Laughlin, copyright 1933 by William Carlos Williams; *The Great American Novel*, copyright 1923 by William Carlos Williams; *The Farmers' Daughters*, copyright 1932 by William Carlos Williams, copyright © 1957 by Florence H. Williams; *White Mule*, copyright 1937 by New Directions Publishing Corporation; *Personae* by Ezra Pound, copyright 1926 by Ezra Pound.

To the memory of my father

Preface

The structure of my argument has some peculiarities and should be justified at the start. My first aim has been to give the reader a sense of both the unity and the range of Williams's writing. My main chapters thus deal with his attempts to renew such standard forms as the lyric poem, historical essay, short story, novel, epic and meditative poem. To handle such a large body of work, my principle has been to select and concentrate and (with just a few exceptions) to select on the basis of quality. But my method of organization turns out to be developmental as well as generic: Williams seems to have proceeded almost systematically from one literary form to the next as his career advanced. In addition, my first two chapters deal with the formative phase of Williams's development, viewing it from both personal and more broadly historical perspectives.

I am grateful to the many scholars, colleagues, and friends who, directly and indirectly, by suggestion and by challenge, have helped me to clarify my ideas. My greatest debt, however, is to my students and my own teachers. Two classes of Berkeley seniors greatly stimulated my thinking about Williams. J.C. Levenson originally prompted my enthusiasm for Williams and he rigorously directed my first writing about Williams. He and Samuel H. Monk are the readers whose standards I would most like to meet.

Completion of my book was facilitated by grants from the American Council of Learned Societies and the Humanities Research Institute at the University of California, Berkeley.

J. E. B.
Berkeley, California
July 1970

Contents

WILLIAM CARLOS WILLIAMS

I

The Quest for Roots:
Williams's Early Development

"The place of my birth is the place where the word
begins." *A Voyage to Pagany*

"Everything exists from the beginning," writes William Carlos
Williams in his *The Great American Novel* (p. 9). The implications of this remark are vast; the consequences of believing
them are radical. From this point of view, all conventional
ways of ordering experience are abstract and empty—dried
husks. Conceptions of time as a linear, historical progression are
false; only the moment is real. The present is the beginning,
and it contains everything: the seed of all life. Williams's career
was a series of attempts to enter this moment; his art, a continuous search for the new forms required for its expression.
Yet, his espousal of the momentary did not send Williams on a
rushed quest across the American continent for novel sensations. He spent all but a few years of his life in Rutherford,
New Jersey, where he worked as a physician. Poetry, he
believed, could only thrive in a landscape familiar to the poet.
In spatial terms, too, everything exists from the beginning;
"the place of my birth is the place where the word begins."
  Still, Williams's acceptance of his own origins came only
after a long and arduous struggle. At first, his family inhibited
his strong sensuality, creating an agonizing division in the boy.
While the opening sections of his *Autobiography* stress the

3

physical exuberance of childhood, there is an undercurrent of
terror throughout. "Terror dominated my youth, not fear,"
Williams says (p. 3). "I was not afraid. I had the normal fears,
naturally, but they could be condoned, not the terror that
flared from the hidden places and all 'heaven.' " In a real sense
the terror he felt did come from heaven—from the rigid idealism and moral perfectionism his parents tried to instill in him.
The mature Williams was to emphasize the physical as the
source of all life; but the idealism of his parents at first made
his earthy instincts frightening to him and, through adolescence and even into early manhood, Williams obediently
sought to distance himself from the corporeal.

These self-divisions were particularly evident at the awakening of his interest in poetry. In 1902, while a student at Horace
Mann High School in New York City, Williams read Whitman's *Leaves of Grass*. In the fall of that year, when he en-
tered the Medical School at the University of Pennsylvania, "I
brought that book with me and I absorbed it with enthusiasm.
I loved to read the poems to myself." [1] He was inspired to fill
a set of notebooks with "quick spontaneous poems" in the
manner of Whitman (*IW*, p. 5). Yet, as he was enthusiastically
absorbing Whitman, he was also reading Keats with a submis-
sive reverence: "Keats, during the years at medical school, was
my God" (*Auto*, p. 53). The result was that at the same time
he was writing rough, free poems after Whitman, he was also
writing what he thought to be suave, polished sonnets after
Keats. The Keatsian poems, in deference to the respectable literary opinion of the time, were those intended for public
view. Granted an interview with his brother's English teacher,
Arlo Bates of M.I.T., the young medical student brought a
Keatsian imitation rather than the notebook poems (*Auto*, pp.
54–55).

"It is curious," Williams later remarked, "that I was so
preoccupied with the studied elegance of Keats on the one
hand and with the raw vigor of Whitman on the other" (*IW*,
p. 8). His divided allegiance is not so curious, however, when
we look at it in the context of the tensions of his adolescence.
The Whitmanesque poems he called "my secret life," suggest-

ing that what was most alive in him was feared and hidden at this point (*IW*, p. 8). It may be, as Eric Erikson argues, that a prolonged period of restraint is necessary to generate revolutionary energy.[2] But between 1902 and 1914, as Williams became the earnest, upright, and remote young man his parents encouraged him to be, he became increasingly impatient with their constraints—from which he dramatically delivered himself by his identification with the physical locality, the "filthy Passaic," announced in "The Wanderer" (1914).

Both of them immigrants—the father an Englishman and the mother a Puerto Rican—Williams's parents had great expectations for their first son. They sent him to Horace Mann and then to medical school at Penn, so that he could achieve acceptance via professional success—the classic pattern of immigrant hopes. At the same time, while the parents were by no means fervently religious, they did impose on the boy a strong sense of propriety and a rigid moral code. Their teachings here were reinforced by the boy's English grandmother, in whose care he was often left and who insisted that he be a "gentleman" (*Auto*, p. 4). At one point, Williams dutifully formulated a project, after Benjamin Franklin, to become morally perfect, and even after he had left home for college, he earnestly assured his mother

> that I never did and never will do a premeditated bad deed in my life. Also that I never have had and never will have anything but the purest and highest and best thoughts about you and Papa, and that if anybody ever says a word contrary to your wishes or high ideals I never fail to fight them to a standstill. . . . I have always tried to do all that you and Papa wished me to do and many times I have done things against my own feelings and convictions because you wanted me to. (*SL*, p. 7)

Both parents, success-minded aliens in the New World, seem in different ways to have been personally remote. The father was often physically absent, away on business trips to Central and South America (*Auto*, p. 14), and the mother, a dreamy individual, was a "medium" who often had hallucinatory fits— heavenly visitations that terrified the young Williams (*Auto*, pp. 15–17). Later, Williams viewed his father as the man Williams himself might have become—as a man who had sacrificed his own feelings and convictions to a rigid sense of duty. In the poem "Adam" the father's fear of the physical banishes him from paradise, converting the lush Caribbean island on which he grew up into a hellish world, filled with terrifying sensual seductions. Behind all of Williams's later animus against the Puritan lies this tough, cold, aloof figure of his father. "He was typically English," Williams, who later became an Anglophobe, said: "too English ever for me to be able to talk with animal to animal" (*YMW*, p. 3; *SL*, p. 127). The mature Williams was even more fascinated with the complex character of his mother, dealing with it in "Eve," "All the Fancy Things," and a brief biography, *Yes, Mrs. Williams;* but the most illuminating statement of what she meant to him in early manhood appears in *I Wanted To Write a Poem:*

> I was conscious of my mother's influence all through this time of writing, her ordeal as a woman and as a foreigner in this country. I've always held her as a mythical figure, remote from me, detached, looking down on an area in which I happened to live, a fantastic world where she was moving as a more or less pathetic figure. Remote, not only because of her Puerto Rican background, but also because of her bewilderment at life in a small town in New Jersey after her years in Paris where she had been an art student. Her interest in art became my interest in art. I was personifying her, her detachment from the world of Rutherford. She seemed an heroic figure, a poetic ideal. I didn't especially admire her; I was attached to her. I had not yet established any sort of independent spirit. (*IW*, p. 16)

Into a largely sterile environment, Mrs. Williams introduced an early and important impetus toward artistic activity. Because of her, Williams was at first interested in painting. But the direction of her influence was not immediately creative, since it inspired a sense of beauty that was dreamily nostalgic; it was she who led him to Keats. Behind all of Williams's later attraction to the elegant, his frequent squeamish distaste for the common, lies the refined and remote figure of his mother. A woman of violent temper, Mrs. Williams was more passionately alive than her husband; but she, too, dreaming of her aristocratic past in Puerto Rico and in Paris, was detached from the ordinary life around her in Rutherford.

Had Williams succumbed to his parents, he might have built a lucrative practice, contributed polite, nostalgic verses to *The New Yorker,* and become a neat, orderly, prosperous physician who would "never think anything / but a white thought" (*CEP,* p. 36). But the frustration created by the seeming acceptance of these ideals was evident not just from the poems it produced, as we shall see shortly, but from the very existence of the Whitman notebooks. They worked, he tells us, as a "sort of purgation and confessional, to clear my head and my heart from turgid obsessions" (*Auto,* p. 53). As Williams prepared a face to meet the faces that he met, these notebooks provided expression for the buried life of the body that he always associated with Whitman. Ultimately, the high aspirations, strict morality, and personal aloofness of his parents worked to reinforce his rebelliousness. Their detachment he later equated with constraint and consequently he felt an intense desire to possess the here and now. "Of mixed ancestry," he once wrote, "I felt from earliest childhood that America was the only home I could ever possibly call my own. I felt that it was expressly founded for me, personally, and that it must be my first business in life to possess it" (*SL,* p. 185). Williams later liked to think of himself as combining his father's tenacity of purpose with his mother's passionate feeling; but to be fully awake and creative, he felt, he had to purge their remote idealism and enter the ordinary life, crude as it might be, of the New Jersey town in which he had been born.

As a step toward liberty, the decision to attend medical school at Penn turned out to be an important one. The journey of the young man from the New Jersey provinces to the city of Philadelphia slowly intensified the conflict between his impulses and the high ideals of his family. In Philadelphia, moreover, Williams discovered such people as Ezra Pound,

H. D., and Charles Demuth, who shared the kinds of feelings
that in Rutherford had made him frightened and isolated. They
shared his desire to create and manifested "a provocative indif-
ference to rule and order which I liked" (*Auto*, p. 68). So encouraged was Williams that he dared to show the Whitman
notebooks to Pound, who promptly denounced them (*IW*, p.
5). As incidents like this must have shown, meeting other artists was also conducive to more precise and more vigorous
self-definition. He sensed a precocity and remoteness about
both H. D. and Pound that made him keep to himself. From
the flamboyant Pound he had a direct perception of the romantic artist as bohemian, about which he had immediate reservations:

> What I could never tolerate in Pound or seek for myself was
> the "side" that went with all his posturings as the poet. To me
> that was the emptiest sort of old hat. Any simpleton, I be-
> lieved, should see at once what that came from; the conflict
> between an aristocracy of birth and that of mind and spirit—
> a silly and unnecessary thing. The poet scorning the other
> made himself ridiculous by imitating that which he despised.
> My upbringing assumed rather the humility and caution of
> the scientist. One was or was not *there*. And if one was there,
> it behooved one to be at one's superlative best, and, apart from
> the achievement, a thing in itself, to live inconspicuously, as
> best it might be possible, and to work single-mindedly for the
> task. Not so sweet Ezra. (*Auto*, p. 58)

Here, as throughout the *Autobiography*, the theatrical egotism
of Pound is set against the innocent humility of the author.
Like all announcements of humility, this one carries its own
egotism. Yet his ambivalent friendship with Pound did eventually help Williams to define his own kind of aspiration—to define the artist as an inconspicuous citizen who, immersing himself in the life of his community, dedicates himself to his
artistic tasks with the impersonality of a scientist.

The only "higher" education he had, Williams's scientific
training was basic in shaping his style of life and art. In the
Autobiography Williams says of his motives as a medical student:

> I would continue medicine, for I was determined to be a poet;
> only medicine, a job I enjoyed, would make it possible for me
> to live and write as I wanted to. . . . My furious wish was to
> be normal, undrunk, balanced in everything. I would marry
> (but not yet!) have children and still write, in fact, therefore
> to write. I would not court disease, live in the slums for the
> sake of art, give lice a holiday. I would not "die for art," but
> live for it, grimly! and work, work, work (like Pop), beat
> the game and be free (like Mom, poor soul!) to write, write
> as I alone should write, for the sheer drunkenness of it, I
> might have added. (*Auto*, p. 51)

These remarks no doubt project the intentions of the mature
on the younger Williams, but they also reveal how important
medicine became in moving Williams away from aestheticism.
The practice of medicine clearly deepened his involvement in
the life of his locality, offering the writer intimate contact
with the lives of its inhabitants and eventually opening up a
new world for literary exploration. Parental ambitions had sent
him to medical school in the first place; but what he learned
there was a way to creativity rather than success.

For medicine was not just a way Williams had of extending
his experience; it profoundly affected the point of view from
which he absorbed experience. To the young man who
dreamed of moral perfection, the study of medicine suggested
the radical imperfection of the flesh and taught him that no
human organism is ever finally cured.

> We recover from some somatic, some bodily "fever" [he
> writes] where as observers we have seen various engagements
> between our battalions of cells playing at this or that lethal
> maneuver with other natural elements. It has been interesting.
> Various sewers or feed-mains have given way here or there
> under pressure: various new patterns have been thrown up for
> us upon the screen of our knowledge. But a cure is absurd,
> as absurd as calling these deployments "diseases." (*Auto*, p.
> 286)

This passage shows how medicine finally shaped Williams's
basic sense that life, once genteel illusions have been stripped
away, is a fierce contest for survival; the body is a dark and vi-

olent place. But the pressures of battle throw up new patterns,
he adds; the arduous struggle to adjust to the physical, terrifying as it may be, does not brutalize—it generates. How perceptions like these might become the source of poetry Williams did not yet know; but meanwhile the study of medicine
clearly supported him in his struggle against the moral idealism
of his parents.[3]

Separation from home and family, the discovery of fellow
artists, the science of medicine itself—all these helped to stir the
independent spirit of the young Williams. But the full liberation of his passionate, physical nature was slow to come about
—as the highly derivative and artificial poems of his first
collection make plain. In 1909, when *Poems* first appeared,
Williams had just completed three years of internship in New
York City; part of the time had been spent in a children's hospital in the violent Hell's Kitchen district of the city. But the
gross actuality of his everyday life—the children, women, doc-
tors, and nurses—could not yet, in Williams's view, generate
poetry. Knowing what we do about this period from the *Autobiography* (pp. 71–105), we get the feeling reading the
1909 *Poems* that at this time Williams, as he says of the citizens of Paterson, walked outside of his own body, unroused.
In 1908 the sources of poetry for Williams were clearly in earlier poetry—mainly Keats and the Elizabethans. The results
were correctly assessed in a letter by Pound: "Individual, original [the book] is not. Great art it is not. Poetic it is . . . but
nowhere I think do you add anything to the poets you have
used as models." [4] Straining after the opulence of Keats or the
grace of the Elizabethans, Williams seems merely awkward
and flat. What is most obviously missing is a unique point of
view which might generate a fresh, inventive use of the language.

Still, certain of the poet's attitudes, especially his conception
of himself, are significant, since they are the very opposite of
the attitudes in his mature work. Williams's first book opens
with characteristic affirmations of Innocence and Simplicity;
but at this point in his career he thinks of them as transcendent

qualities, of "heavenly birth," preserved by a precious remoteness from the here and now (*Poems*, p. 7). For the most part the poems either praise abstractions, personified as goddesses, or they pay court to a distant, lovely lady. In either case, the attitude of the poet before the female—the "poetic ideal" he identified with his mother—is reverential, while he views mundane reality with a superior disdain. Implicitly, female or poetic beauty is defined as something rare and distant, ethereal and indistinct. Desire and creativity, which torment as they delight, are activities of the mind, not the "foul and gritty" body (*Poems*, p. 13). "True having lives but only in the mind," the sententious young aesthete declares in "The Quest of Happiness" and in an exhausted idiom which undermines the request as it is made, he prays, "Then loose ye all, ye earthly bonds which cling / About my heart, and—life's new song, begin!"

In accordance with such Platonic aspirations, the poet looks upon himself as an outcast and wanderer; he constantly yearns for "everlasting peace" in some far-off, unobtainable realm (*Poems*, p. 14). Plainly, the melancholy author of this volume is not an ordinary mortal, but one whose vision of the ideal makes him A Man Set Apart. But in spite of the insistence upon the uniqueness of the author, the poet who emerges from this collection is one who is entirely dependent—dependent emotionally upon the remote and lofty figure of his mother as a mythical female ideal and dependent artistically upon Keats and the Elizabethans.

These tendencies are all illustrated in "The Uses of Poetry," a sonnet dedicated to H. D. (whom Williams later recalled as an airy creature whose feet never seemed to touch the ground). The poem's language is flat and awkward; but it is worth looking at closely to establish Williams's personal and poetic identity at this point in his development.

> I've fond anticipation of a day
> O'erfilled with pure diversion presently,
> For I must read a lady poesy
> The while we glide by many a leafy bay,

Hid deep in rushes, where at random play
The glossy black winged May-flies, or whence flee
Hush-throated nestlings in alarm,
Whom we have idly frightened with our boat's long sway.

For, lest o'ersaddened by such woes as spring
To rural peace from our meek onward trend,
What else more fit? We'll draw the light latch-string

And close the door of sense; then satiate wend,
On Poesy's transforming giant wing,
To worlds afar whose fruits all anguish mend.

Very simply, the poet yearns to "close the door of sense"—to transcend the flesh—and drift off into some sheltered domain of "rural peace" and "pure diversion." In a similar way, the poem itself lifts us away from sense experience. Williams's later poems attempt to put us inside immediate experience, but he here tries to enclose and formalize the moment. There is the closed, conventional form of the sonnet. Moreover, with the use of epithets such as "leafy bay," "rural peace" and "hush-throated nestlings," and of inversions such as "whose fruits all anguish mend," Williams deliberately adopts a language that is artificial and literary. The sentence structure—especially the elaborate subordination of the first sentence—shows too that the speaker is not rendering the process of experience but is stepping back, to achieve a polished, finished mode of artistic expression. This distant relation to subject, along with the identification of the beautiful with the remote and the artificial, suggest a use of poetry antithetical to that advocated by the later Williams, who renounced all established forms like the sonnet and argued for a new poetry in the spoken idiom—both as part of his program to jolt his readers out of their yearnings for dreamy tranquility, unlock the doors of their senses, and place them in loving contact with the actual.

Four years after his first volume of poems—in March 1913—Williams was outraged by Harriet Monroe's suggested revisions of two metrically irregular poems. "The poet," he wrote to her,

comes forward assailing the trite and the established, while
the editor is to sheer off all roughness and extravagance. . . .
Now life is above all things else at any moment subversive of
life as it was the moment before—always new, irregular. Verse
to be alive must have infused into it something of the same
order, some tincture of disestablishment, something in the
nature of an impalpable revolution, an ethereal reversal, let
me say. . . . *Poetry* I saw accepting verse of this kind: that is,
verse with perhaps nothing else in it but life—this alone,
regardless of possible imperfections, for no new thing comes
through perfect. (*SL*, pp. 23–24)

The assertive tone of this letter from an unrecognized poet to
the editor of *Poetry* reveals a new spirit of confidence in the
writer; Williams has now envisioned the creative act as a process in which constricting conventions are broken apart in
order to release the instincts of the individual artist. Independence, revolution, chaos are now all part of his program for
life and art. Still, the poems of this period, most of them collected in *The Tempers* (1913), remain largely derivative, with
Ezra Pound replacing John Keats as the chief model. If Williams was moving toward an abstract definition of art as an ex-
perimental process, he continued to write poems that sought to
provide conventional subjects with new verbal finish. His
practice, while often deliberately rougher than in 1909, still
equated art with rhetorical polish rather than self-expression.

The feeling that generates much of Pound's work in this period is the melancholy of the outcast. Characteristically, he
sees himself as an urbane, weary courtier oppressed by the vul-
garities of his bourgeois age. Similarly fatigued by the wintry
environment of the modern world, Williams expresses *tristitia
post coitum* in "Postlude," a mournful persistence in the face
of futility in "Ad Infinitum," a feeling of impotence in "Crude
Lament," and the stylized weariness of "An After Song" :

> So art thou broken in upon me, Apollo,
> Through a splendor of purple garments—
> Held by the yellow-haired Clymene
> To clothe the white of thy shoulders—

Bare from the day's leaping of horses.
This is strange to me, here in the modern twilight.

As in the 1909 poems, the beautiful is identified with the remote, here the lost world of the past. The immediate experience, the observation of the sunset, will not suffice for poetry.
Such a commonplace occurrence is infused with poetic significance only by lifting it into the rare world of classical myth.
Contemporary experience, neatly shaped into the form of the
classical epigram, is rendered by a deliberately archaic language and imagery. Lyric nostalgia, although now mixed with
irony, remains the dominant mood. The myth informing this
poem, contrasting the radiant past with the "modern twilight,"
is not the myth of growth but of decline.

Still, there were signs of progress. Williams's observation
that "certain poems in *The Tempers*, or perhaps just certain
lines in some of the poems, show that I was beginning to turn
away from the romantic" is true enough if we understand "romantic" to mean the remote (*IW*, p. 17). On the whole, these
poems do show a greater range and vigor of feeling than the
1909 volume. In "Mezzo Forte" a dramatic lyric which begins
"Take that, damn you; and that!" we have a strong feeling ex-
pressed in strong speech, although the angry defiance is a literary convention as old as the Petrarchanism it mocks. "The
Death of Franco of Cologne: His Prophecy of Beethoven," a
dramatic monologue after Browning, is declamatory in style
but its argument prefigures the mature Williams. Williams
praises Franco of Cologne, who invented our system of musical
notation, over Beethoven, who worked to mastery within it;
this adumbrates Williams's later insistence upon rough inven-
tiveness over formal perfection. "Con Brio" works out some of
the more radical implications in this shift. There, for the first
time in his work, Williams denounces repression and calls for
an emotional spontaneity and openness. In these last two poems
the young poet is asserting an expressive rather than a rhetorical view of art. To this extent, he had become more, not less,
romantic. But except for the use of the colloquial voice in a

few poems, there is little sense that poetry can be generated
out of contact with the immediate. Invention, experiment, release are, importantly, advocated; but it is still, in the language
of the letter to Miss Monroe, in the nature of an *impalpable*
revolution, an *ethereal* reversal.

By imitating Pound, Williams learned he could not with
conviction write the kind of smooth, concentrated, highly finished song his friend had mastered. He also learned, it appears,
what he did not want to be: he was no courtier, but a plain,
inconspicuous inhabitant of the ordinary world. "Contemporania," the most direct poetic tribute to Pound in *The Tempers,*
also asserts Williams's awareness of the fundamental difference
between Pound and himself.

> Contemporania
> The corner of a great rain
> Steamy with the country
> Has fallen upon my garden.
>
> I go back and forth now
> And the little leaves follow me
> Talking of the great rain,
> Of branches broken,
> And the farmer's curses!
>
> But I go back and forth
> In this corner of a garden
> And the green shoots follow
> Praising the great rain.
>
> We are not curst together,
> The leaves and I,
> Framing devices, flower devices
> And other ways of peopling
> The barren country.
> Truly it was a very great rain
> That makes the little leaves follow me.

This somewhat enigmatic poem becomes clearer once we remember that "Contemporania" was the general title for a
group of eleven poems which Pound published in *Poetry,*

April 1913. Williams's "great rain" from the "country" and his "flower devices" allude to one of these poems by Pound, "Salutation the Second" :

> You were praised, my books,
>   because I had just come from the country;
> I was twenty years behind the times
>   so you found an audience ready.
> I do not disown you,
>   do not disown your progeny.
>
> Here they stand without quaint devices,
> Here they are with nothing archaic about them.

As he goes on, Pound makes clear he is announcing his own liberation from the genteel tradition; he enjoins his new irreverent songs to defy the oppressive propriety of his audience:

> Ruffle the skirts of prudes,
>   speak of their knees and ankles,
> But, above all, go to practical people—
>   go! jangle their door-bells!
> Say that you do no work
>   and that you will live forever.

Dissatisfied with the genteel mask of the courtier, Pound here proclaims a reversal of aim and method from his earlier work. His new songs, he says, are to be rough and exuberant—"impudent and naked"—not smoothly fashioned in "quaint devices." Thus, in "Salutation the Second" we encounter not the urbane control of the aristocrat but the scornful defiance of the bohemian and expatriate. Still, the assumptions are elitist: Pound is not so much trying to jolt the Philistine awake as he is sharing his scorn with an audience of those who are already saved.

In his own "Contemporania" Williams is acknowledging an important debt to this new Pound. While the "great rain" in his poem can mean any violent innovation, the literary allusions indicate that Williams is specifically praising Pound for his role in breaking up established human and literary orders. Unlike the practical farmer who curses the disruption of routine, the Williams of "Contemporania" rejoices in chaos. In fact, the liberating shift from a fixed, constraining order to a fertile chaos was shortly to become a major subject of Williams's verse and Pound clearly helped him to find it. But if Williams here declares an affinity with Pound the revolutionary, he also expresses the reservations he had felt about the egotistical bohemian from their first encounters in Philadelphia. Williams's "Contemporania" acknowledges a debt, but it also defines a basic difference.

Both Pound and Williams want to move away from the artificial "quaint devices" of their earlier work. But Williams's desire to frame "flower devices" suggests a conception of himself as quite different from Pound. In "Salutation the Second" Pound speaks derisively, as the expatriate; in "Contemporania" Williams speaks in the familiar voice of a townsman. The gardener of his poem, a humble and amiable citizen, seeks not to provoke the wrath of his audience but to nurture growth in his "barren country." The poet is thus a modest and commonplace figure—with prophetic ambitions: he enters the ordinary world in order to regenerate it, to release the creative powers buried in his fellow citizens. Such an act of release requires the violent breaking apart of fixed modes of thought and feeling; it requires self-reliance. But this liberation is only the beginning of the process of renewal. "Only he is lost who has been cut off from his fellows," Williams believed (*SE*, p. 186). But the repressed bodily forces that Williams wants to release are shared by all men, and so their liberation draws men together, by asserting what is common. The aesthete impoverishes himself by cutting himself off from his fellows and becomes a mirror image of their isolation and impotence. The democratic poet, by the very act which accomplishes his independence, achieves communion with his fellows; self-reliance leads to fraternal contact.

The radical shift evident in just a few of *The Tempers* poems had already been acted out in Williams's life. In 1909 Williams had returned briefly to Rutherford, where his first book was published and where he met Florence Herman, later his wife. The couple were engaged for three years—"I had to

do a lot of readjusting to come out softened down for marriage," he later said (*Auto*, p. 129)—and before settling down
he left, in early 1910, for a year in Europe. Most of this time
was spent studying medicine in Leipzig, but the high point of
the trip was a visit with Pound in Kensington. There, he was
exposed to an "intense literary atmosphere" which he found
"thrilling, every minute of it," but "fatiguing in the extreme"
(*Auto*, p. 117). Importantly, he felt that the effect of his arduous duties as a physician was precisely the reverse. The
writer could experience a profound regeneration through his
medical practice—because in the very intensity of his identification with the patient's struggle, he could escape the turgid
obsessions of his own life.

> I lost myself in the very properties of their minds [he says of
> his patients]: for the moment at least I actually became *them*,
> whoever they should be, so that when I detached myself from
> them at the end of a half-hour of intense concentration over
> some illness which was affecting them, it was as though I were
> reawakening from a sleep. For the moment I myself did not
> exist, nothing of myself affected me. As a consequence I came
> back to myself, as from any other sleep, refreshed. (*Auto*, p.
> 356)

Typically, Williams here conceives of integration as a movement in and out of the self in a continuous process of renewal
—a process that is thwarted by the rarefied atmosphere of the
literary world. And so when he returned here in 1911, he was
purging himself of aestheticism and identifying himself with
the common ground of his locality. Within a few years—by
early 1913—he had been married, bought a large old house, set
up medical practice and become a father. Life in these banal
surroundings was certainly not without its tensions, but these
pressures would, Williams hoped, generate authentic creativity.
     Influencing these changes in Williams were a variety of
forces. As we shall see, in addition to the direct impact of
Pound, such matters as the Paterson silk strike of 1913 and the
sense of a widespread insurgency in the arts generated by the

Armory Show and the arrival of the New Poetry must be taken into account. But of deep importance for Williams was a new reading of *Leaves of Grass*. On the first of March 1913, just two weeks before he advocated "roughness and extravagance" to Harriet Monroe, Williams received a copy of Whitman's poetry from his wife. Now owned by the library at the University of Pennsylvania, this book, which falls open to the beginning of "Song of Myself," has obviously been read many times, although it has not been marked in a way that would suggest detailed study. What the condition of the book suggests is that Whitman exerted little stylistic influence on Williams, who later wrote that "the only way to be like Whitman is to write *unlike* Whitman." [5] What Whitman helped Williams to do was to root himself in the here and now and release those creative energies repressed by his family and society—so that he could begin to learn to write like William Carlos Williams.

Throughout his career—in "America, Whitman, and the Art of Poetry" (1917), in "An Essay on *Leaves of Grass*" (1955), and in numerous comments in letters and essays—Williams asserted his debt to Whitman and made clear that what he had derived was not a literary style, but a bold conception of his poetic task.[6] Keats, whose style he had imitated, Williams remembered as a "God" (*Auto*, p. 53); Whitman, who helped him to be himself, Williams remembered as a comrade with whom he had "an instinctive drive to get in touch." [7] What brought the two poets together was their self-reliant need to break apart conventional poetic forms in order to release *their* passions, and their belief that these secret passions were shared by their audience. In the opening lines of "Song of Myself," we hear, Williams wrote, "the cry of a man breaking through the barriers of constraint IN ORDER TO BE ABLE TO SAY *exactly* what was in his mind." [8] In Williams's view, Whitman was "tremendously important in the history of modern poetry" because he

> broke through the deadness of copied forms which keep shouting above everything that wants to get said today drown-

ing out one man with the accumulated weight of a thousand
voices in the past—re-establishing the tyrannies of the past, the
very tyrannies that we are seeking to diminish. The structure
of the old is active, it says no! to everything in propaganda and
poetry that wants to say yes. Whitman broke through that.
That was basic and good. (*SE*, p. 218)

Only occasionally, Williams believed, had Whitman been able
to recombine successfully the fragments he had freed. Whitman had "composed 'freely,' he followed his untrammeled ne-
cessity. What he did not do was to study what he had done, to
go over it, to select and reject, which is the making of the artist" (*SE*, p. 230). But Whitman's "barbaric yawp" did return
us to the simple, unformed elements of poetry and perception,
the place where we must begin. Pound, conceding in his fa-
mous "Pact" that Whitman had broken new wood, believed
that the modern task was to carve and polish; Williams wanted
to re-enact fully the process of release and re-formation that
Whitman had started. After his reading of Whitman in 1913,
Williams identified not the suave manipulation of conventional
attitudes but the passionate expression of feeling as the proper
business of poetry.

Whitman thus helped Williams both to discover and to af-
firm his creative powers; but in 1913 it was no longer quite
possible to assume a personal omnipotence and simply let go.
The poet who grew up in the expansive Age of Jackson could
easily leap free of oppressive conventions—as Whitman does in
the opening sections of "Song of Myself"; but for Williams,
who grew up after the closing of the frontier and during a period of savage industrial exploitation, the self no longer seemed
quite so omnipotent. His early poems, we have seen, assume
impotence and yearn for flight. But in the poems written after
1914 Williams's theme is the power of the marginal or embattled self to break through restrictions and generate new
growth: "Saxifrage," he said, "is my flower that splits / the
rocks" (*CLP*, p. 7). The new Williams is brought forth in
"The Wanderer," published in early 1914. In this poem, crucial to any study of his development, Williams examines his
personal and poetic development, renounces the dreamy ideal-

> of flames. So be it. A bottle, mauled
> by the flames, belly-bent with laughter:
> yellow, green. So be it—of drunkenness
> survived, in guffaws of flame. All fire afire!
> So be it. Swallowing the fire. So be
> it. Torqued to laughter by the fire,
> the very fire. So be it. Chortling at flames
> sucked in, a multiformity of laughter, a
> flaming gravity surpassing the sobriety of
> flames, a chastity of annihilation. Recreant,
> calling it good. Calling the fire good.
> So be it. The beauty of fire-blasted sand
> that was glass, that was a bottle: unbottled.
> Unabashed. So be it.   (p. 142)

The bottle, literally bent by the flames, is not imagined as wracked, tortured by the experience, but as letting go a howl of release, a near hysterical laughter. "Hell's fire" is not pure negation, it is a destructive / creative force which can produce the sort of primal metamorphosis it does here. The flames annihilate form—unbottle the bottle—and then, after rendering it fluid, create a new shape. Like the girl in the "white lace dress," the bottle is battered, a drunken force runs through it, but the "old bottle, mauled by the fire / gets a new glaze, the glass warped / to a new distinction, reclaiming the / undefined." Line endings here stress the unexpected turn, the creative reversal, in the process, as what is "mauled" gets a "new glaze," what is "warped" receives a "new distinction," just as the girl's busted nose marks her as "credible," a truly beautiful thing. It is through this kind of ordeal, surrender to these terrifying forces, that ultimately comes the purity Paterson has been searching for. Moreover, from Book I glass has been associated with the rigid, egotistical side of Paterson's character—as in "the regularly ordered plateglass of / his thoughts." So what happens to the bottle happens to Paterson's mind, too. He speaks of "hottest / lips lifted till no shape but a vast / molt of the news flows. Drink / of the news, fluid to the breath." Literally the "hottest lips" refer to the shape of the molten glass, but they are also the lips of the poet, burning with passion, as

he drinks in the news of metamorphosis. "Molt" is a pun, referring both to "molten" and to "moulting," and as Paterson's
plateglass mind is made fluid by a drunken emotion, he passes
into a new phase of his life. Yet both bottle and poet finally
triumph over the fire by making a transient moment of passion
eternal. After the blaze the glass is "splotched with concentric
rainbows / of cold fire" just as an experience of passion can be
frozen, forever, in the words of a poem. The bottle is "deflowered, reflowered," "mauled / to a new distinction." At the
end, the passage turns comically back on itself, with Paterson
now hysterically laughing at the fire.

> Hell's fire. Fire. Sit your horny ass
> down. What's your game? Beat you
> at your own game, Fire. Outlast you:
> Poet Beats Fire at Its Own Game! The bottle!
> the bottle! the bottle! the bottle! I
> give you the bottle! What's burning
> now, Fire?

The answer to that emphatically placed "now" is, of course,
the bottle—*and* the language in which the poet has caught the
process of its recreation (pp. 142–43).

An advance from Paterson's state of mind in the "descent
beckons" passage is quite clear, if "advance" is the right word
for a step which takes him right into the process of disintegration. But in the poem's characteristic manner, even this moment of triumph—when what is deflowered, reflowers eternally
—is ripped apart. From a celebration of the power of the poet
to "outlast" the fire, Paterson modulates to an acknowledgment of his own inadequate responsiveness and his inability to
catch the flame's mysterious movements in language. This
humbler mood takes him, at the end of Book III, Part II (pp.
150–52), to memory of an episode with a black woman, another manifestation of the Beautiful Thing. Paterson encounters her below the ground, in a basement, "by the laundry
tubs,"

in a low bed (waiting)
under the mud plashed windows among the scabrous
dirt of the holy sheets   .

Like the mauled bottle and the marked girl, she is "scarred"
(by whips), but indifferent and accepting—silently dignified.

.   a docile queen, not bothered
to stick her tongue out at the moon, indifferent,
through loss, but   .

queenly,
in bad luck, the luck of the stars, the black stars

.   the night of a mine

Although she is surrounded by dirt and ugliness, she does
not, as Paterson often does, lapse into despair or anxiety; she
remains loose, relaxed, "stretched out negligently on the dirty
sheet." As Paterson perceives, this dark woman in the squalid
basement is "Persephone / gone to hell"—regal in her indiffer-
ence, radiant in the surrounding darkness. She gives us another
of the third book's images of hell experienced, beaten, sur-
vived.

When Paterson first remembers her in Part I, he recalls an
incident in which he had been brutally puritannical with her.

(Then, my anger rising) TAKE OFF YOUR
CLOTHES! I didn't ask you
to take off your skin . I said your
clothes, your clothes. You smell
like a whore. I ask you to bathe in my
opinions, the astonishing virtue of your
lost body (I said)   .   (pp. 128–29)

This passage shows how Paterson, in his demands for a pure
beauty, is himself implicated in the maiming and violating of
natural beauty. But in Part II he recounts a subsequent episode
when he was open, receptive to the power of this woman.

—for I was overcome
by amazement and could do nothing but admire
and lean to care for you in your quietness—

    who looked at me, smiling, and we remained
    thus looking, each at the other   .   in silence   .

    You lethargic, waiting upon me, waiting for
    the fire and I
            attendant upon you, shaken by your beauty

    Shaken by your beauty   .
                            Shaken.

Paterson is here humble, awed, "attendant," "shaken." Instead
of trying to force his righteous opinions upon her "lost body,"
he lets her physical being speak silently to him, and her care-
less, lethargic manner—a power that comes across without asserting itself—has much to teach him. At this crucial moment
of encounter between the hero and the object of his torturous
quest, we might expect a high-pitched scene of climax; but it is
the whole point of this meeting that it be quietly played
down, flattened out. The surrender of the desire for artistic
mastery and the capacity to be shaken go hand in hand for Paterson (pp. 150–52). This scene is at several levels of intensity
below the "drunken" pitch of the episode of the mauled bottle, and by the end of Part II, Paterson has dropped to a still
more modest tone.

                I can't be half gentle enough,
        half tender enough
                    toward you, toward you,
        inarticulate, not half loving enough

        BRIGHTen
                    the cor
                            ner
        where   you   are!
                        —a flame,
            black plush, a dark flame.   (p. 154)

At this key moment, words fail the inarticulate poet; not half
gentle or tender enough, they too whip and scar the Beautiful
Thing. But this admission of failure and guilt is exactly the
kind of limited triumph available to Paterson. There is so

much for him to discard, so much to be cut away, that he cannot wholly reconstitute himself; what he can do is relax, give
up the partial victories of art and open himself to the beauty
that is before him.

Searching for beauty in the refined atmosphere of the library, Paterson discovers it living in a dirty basement; as always in Williams, beauty is a flame in the underworld—the radiant gist hidden in the pitch blend. But the flood of Part III
takes Paterson down even further into the darkness and filth in
which he must begin.

                        Upon which there intervenes
          a sour stench of embers. So be it. Rain
          falls and surfeits the river's upper reaches,
          gathering slowly. So be it. Draws together,
          runnel by runnel. So be it. A broken oar
          is found by the searching waters. Loosened
          it begins to move. So be it. Old timbers
          sigh—and yield. The well that gave sweet water
          is sullied. So be it. And lilies that floated
          quiet in the shallows, anchored, tug as
          fish at a line. So be it. And are by their
          stems pulled under, drowned in the muddy flux.
          The white crane flies into the wood.
          So be it. Men stand at the bridge, silent,
          watching. So be it. So be it.

The tornado and fire are wild forces that can quickly be felt as
liberating, but the flood is heavy and oppressive, sullying clear
waters, burying all in a "muddy flux." Moreover, as soon as
the flood is introduced as natural fact, it is given a symbolic
sense—referring to the mass of books in which Paterson has
been immersing himself.

                        And there rises
          a counterpart, of reading, slowly, overwhelming
          the mind; anchors him in his chair. So be
          it. He turns   .   O Paradiso! The stream
          grows leaden within him, his lilies drag. So
          be it. Texts mount and complicate them-

> selves, lead to further texts and those
> to synopses, digests and emendations. So be it.
> Until the words break loose or—sadly
> hold, unshaken. Unshaken! So be it. For
> the made-arch holds, the water piles up debris
> against it but it is unshaken. They gather
> upon the bridge and look down, unshaken.
> So be it. So be it. So be it.   (p. 156)

Anchored to his chair in the library, Paterson at one point seems to turn away and look for relief ("O Paradiso!"), but is only turning another page. His inventive powers grow leaden, his spirit drags; he's read too much. And as books pile up, they get further and further from immediate experience—"until the words break loose"; the end of this progressive fading away from the sources of writing is sheer chaos, which is a new beginning. The alternatives for Paterson are to let this process of disintegration run its course ("So be it") or to try to build barriers against it, to get outside and above it, like the men on the bridge who watch silently, unshaken (p. 156).

Through most of Part III the waters continue to rise—"to the teeth, to the very eyes" becomes a refrain—covering all signs of life with their muddy flux. At moments Paterson wants to "*do*" something to turn against this oppressive force—

> But somehow a man must lift himself
> again—
>   again is the magic word   .
>   turning the in out   :
> Speed against the inundation (p. 162)

—but the hopelessness of this counter-thrust is suggested by the image of the fish "at full speed / stationary / in the leaping stream" (p. 163). Eventually, on page 164, words do break loose: random bits of conversation, reading, signs from a florist shop, reflections by the poet slant down the page in several directions. The poem sinks, breaks free of the regularly ordered lines of typography. On the adjacent page appears a letter from Pound, recommending more reading, more civilization. But his experience with the leaden flood of books

prompts Paterson to opt for spontaneity. At the start of Part
III, in answer to a voice urging a cautious perfectionism
("watch carefully and erase"), he declares: "write carelessly so
that nothing that is not green will survive" (p. 155). More and
more the embattled Paterson comes to identify art not with
decorum but the release of this living force.

The flood continues to rise until it reaches

> —to the teeth, to the very eyes
> .   uh,   uh
> ### FULL STOP
>
> —and leave the world
> to darkness
> and to
> me

But then as the waters ebb, Paterson, left in the post-alluvial
muck, falls into one of the most despairing moments of the entire poem:

> When the water has receded most things have lost their
> form. They lean in the direction the current went. Mud
> covers them
>
> —fertile(?)mud.
>
> If it were only fertile. Rather a sort of muck, a detritus,
> in this case—a pustular scum, a decay, a choking
> lifelessness—that leaves the soil clogged after it,
> that glues the sandy bottom and blackens stones—so that
> they have to be scoured three times when, because of
> an attractive brokenness, we take them up for garden uses.
> An acrid, a revolting stench comes out of them, almost one
> might say a granular stench—fouls the mind   .
>
> How to begin to find a shape—to begin to begin again,
> turning the inside out : to find one phrase that will
> lie married beside another for delight   .   ?
> —seems beyond attainment   .
>
> *American poetry is a very easy subject to discuss for the*
> *simple reason that it does not exist*   (p. 167)

As a result of the flood, Paterson the city and Paterson the man in the library are both buried in a heavy, stinking, life-choking mud; foulness covers everything. At such moments, artistic activity seems impossible. Yet, like the young poet in "The Wanderer," the man-city has gone through an immersion in foulness, a reduction to formlessness—a descent to the primal ooze which is at the start of all things. Language begins anew at the point where speech falls to an inarticulate "uh"; art begins again at the point where art ends. With the "FULL STOP" Paterson is left in a kind of graveyard—thus the allusion to Gray's "Elegy"—but left, alone and free, in the creative darkness.

So, at the bottommost point of despair, lines suddenly tighten, mood abruptly turns upward. This is exactly the kind of reversal we have seen happening again and again in the poem; it cannot be explained rationally, it results from no act of conscious will on the part of Paterson, but simply from the natural life of feelings, a process in which moods build, disintegrate, generate their opposites. By now we are prepared to accept this as the "logic" of Paterson's mind, and thus of the poem—and so is Paterson. In fact, the rise of feeling here is equated with his acceptance of natural processes: now that the flood has run its course, Paterson is willing to turn the task of renewal over to the digestive processes of the earth.

> Degraded. The leaf torn from
> the calendar. All forgot. Give
> it over to the woman, let her
> begin again—with insects
> and decay, decay and then insects :
> the leaves—that were varnished
> with sediment, fallen, the clutter
> made piecemeal by decay, a
> digestion takes place   .
>
> —of this, make it of *this*, this
> this, this, this, this   . (pp. 167–68)

This is a crucial moment in the poem, for Paterson, having experienced a series of agonizing and humiliating ordeals, nevertheless asserts a faith that creation issues from destruction. The degradation has ripped away the accumulations of calendar time and actually cleaned his mind: "all forgot." Antithetical to his own immersion in these painful processes is the detachment of the men who coldly watch from the bridge—a remoteness that Paterson identifies with T. S. Eliot. "Who was it spoke of April?" he asks. "Some / insane engineer." The bridge is a metaphor for technical mastery of any kind, including a poetic one, that is achieved by abstraction from the processes of nature. "Loosen the flesh / from the machine," Paterson proclaims, "build no more / bridges." Instead of seeking technical perfection, "let the words / fall any way at all—that they may / hit love aslant"—as they do on the chaotic page 164. "They want to rescue too much, / the flood," annihilating the works of engineers, "has done its work" (p. 169).

As Paterson now recognizes, the marriage of form and energy he envisioned at the start of the poem could be realized "in a hundred years, perhaps," but at the moment a rough, flagrant vitality is all he can hope for. Rather than the attainment of formal mastery, the writer must begin by breaking apart fixed modes; but the collapse of his artistic aspirations takes Paterson back to the origins of art in the formless moment. And so at the end of Book III, he abandons the library and returns to the Falls.

> The past above, the future below
> and the present pouring down: the roar,
> the roar of the present, a speech—
> is, of necessity, my sole concern   .
>
> They plunged, they fell in a swoon   .
> or by intention, to make an end—the
> roar, unrelenting, witnessing   .
> Neither the past nor the future
>
> Neither to stare, amnesic—forgetting.
> The language cascades into the
> invisible, beyond and above : the falls
> of which it is the visible part—

Not until I had made of it a replica
will my sins be forgiven and my
disease cured—in wax: *la capella di S. Rocco*
on the sandstone crest above the old

copper mines—where I used to see
the images of arms and knees
hung on nails (de Montpellier) .
No meaning. And yet, unless I find a place

apart from it, I am its slave,
its sleeper, bewildered—dazzled
by distance . I cannot stay here
to spend my life looking into the past:

the future's no answer. I must
find my meaning and lay it, white,
beside the sliding water: myself—
comb out the language—or succumb

—whatever the complexion. Let
me out! (Well, go!) this rhetoric
is real! (pp. 172–73)

Paterson reflects on the dilemmas that have beset him throughout the poem. Meaning, he here decides, cannot be found in library or church, past or future, but must be combed out of
the undifferentiated chaos of the present. Whatever its complexion, the physical world must be the source of any common
language or mythology. Yet man cannot simply lose himself in
the "roar" of immediacy: he can not stare amnesic, like Mrs.
Cumming, forgetting the self in yearning for union with nature. The self is here identified in terms of a tension between
mind and matter, form and actuality—but with most emphasis
on the present need for the mind to refresh its contact with
physical experience. The Falls, again, stands for the core of
creative energy shared by all the citizens of Paterson, but forgotten in the ambitions, distractions of modern industrial life.
To redeem himself and his city, the poet must create a replica
of this forgotten power, a verbal object that is different from
the Falls but preserving its beauty and force. Earlier in Book
III Paterson claims that "the writing is nothing, the being / in

a position to write (that's // where they get you) is nine
tenths / of the difficulty . . ." (p. 137). Most of his energy
goes into breaking forms down, getting back to the sources of
art; mastery seems beyond attainment. But by the end of Book
III he has maneuvered himself into a position to write, and that
position, characteristic for Williams, is at the *edge* of the Falls,
place of maximum exposure to the risks, and to the power, of
raw experience. At last Paterson has begun.

Book IV takes us down into some of the poem's most hellish
experiences in the ironic "An Idyll" of Part I, only to lift us
into its most visionary mood in Part II's celebration of Ma-
dame Curie as the creative principle. This descent/ascent pattern is also exemplified in Part III, originally intended to be
Paterson's final episode. The title for Book IV is "The Run to
the Sea," and in this last section Paterson follows the Passaic
down past Manhattan to its end, and its origin, in the Atlantic.
Here the sea is anything but the gentle, buoyant element we
find in a writer like Emerson; it is brute nature, unordered and
shark-infested. At moments the sea becomes "our nostalgic /
mother in whom the dead, enwombed again / cry out to us to
return . / the blood dark sea" (p. 236). This pull toward nostalgia becomes especially strong as Paterson, now quite old, en-
gages in extensive reminiscences of old friends, lovers, his
mother, a visit to Haiti and the history of his town. The blood
dark sea is death, and Paterson appears to be slowly, helplessly,
sinking into it. He stutters hopelessly at one point: "—you cannot believe / that it can begin again, again, here / again . here"
(p. 234).

Yet, if the sea is death, it is also birth, the origin of life.
Among "the scum / and wrack . among the brown fronds /
and limp starfish," says Paterson, "seeds float in" (p. 235); the
sea is another hell he must endure to recover the seeds of Persephone. For this reason both voices in the debate near the
close of the poem—"the sea is not our home," "you must
come to it"—are right. The debate precedes a swim Paterson
takes in the Atlantic. He goes so far out that he is no longer
recognizably human—he dies into the scene. Yet the episode
ends not with the swimmer being swept helplessly out to sea,

but with his return to the beach where he naps briefly, rises, puts on a pair of faded overalls and a shirt with its sleeves still rolled up, picks some beach plums and heads inland accompanied by his dog (pp. 236–38). He has come to the sea, but it is not his home. The seeds turned up by this process of renewal must be planted in the earth. Moreover, this solitary and carefree rough is headed, Williams tells us, "toward Camden where Walt Whitman, much traduced, lived the latter years of his life and died" (*Auto*, p. 392). This figure is identified with Whitman, Paterson, and the younger poet A. G. (Allen Ginsberg) whose work shows, as he tells Paterson in a letter, that "at least one actual citizen of your community has inherited your experience in his struggle to love and know his world-city, through your work, which is an accomplishment you almost cannot have hoped to achieve" (p. 205). The seed of creativity persists through time; the wanderer heading inland is an archetypal figure. At its close, the poem affirms that the quest for beginnings is an eternal one.

Shortly before finishing the fourth book Williams wrote to a friend,

> A man wonders why he bothers to continue to write. And yet it is precisely then that to write is most imperative for us. That, if I can do it, will be the end of *Paterson*, Book IV. The ocean of savage lusts in which the wounded shark gnashes at his own tail is not our home. It is the seed that floats to shore, one word, one tiny even microscopic word, is that which can alone save us. (*SL*, p. 292)

At the end of "The Waste Land" Tiresias makes a similarly modest claim: "These fragments I have shored against my ruins." But the difference between these two poems is basic. "The Waste Land" is a kind of anti-epic, a poem in which the quest for meaning is entirely thwarted and we are left, at the end, waiting for the collapse of western civilization. *Paterson* is a pre-epic, showing that the process of disintegration releases forces that can build a new world. It confronts, again and again, the savagery of contemporary society, but still affirms a creative seed. Eliot's end is Williams's beginning.

VII

A Celebration of the Light

"The serpent // has its tail in its mouth / AGAIN!"
Paterson V

In 1954 Williams published *The Desert Music and Other Poems*, a book that announced a new departure in his career. To the author himself the book was "special" because it contained the first poems in which he employed his new "variable foot" (*IW*, pp. 88–89). But a reader coming to these poems across the whole course of Williams's development will recognize that the new line is simply one manifestation of a pervasive shift of style and point of view. The earlier poems are remarkable for their toughness and spontaneity, their intensity and fluidity, their disciplined objectification of personal feeling. But in the poetry of *The Desert Music, Journey to Love* (1955), *Paterson* V (1958) and *Pictures from Brueghel* (1962) we discover an easy, measured grace, a tone of relaxed assurance, tenderness and benignity of feeling, a manner that is openly discursive and personal. The need to break things apart has gone; the aging poet, content with his long and productive life, speaks out in a tone of sagacity and pulls the diverse parts of his experience into unity.

As Williams writes in *Paterson* V, "The (self) direction has been changed" (*P*, p. 271). His use of the passive voice is exact: the new direction his work took in the 1950's was not the result of any act of volition, it grew out of a new set of circumstances that were thrust on him. In March, 1951—as he was finishing his *Autobiography*—Williams suffered a severe apoplectic stroke.[1] He almost died, temporarily lost the power of speech, was forced into a prolonged period of recuperation and, eventually, into retirement from his medical practice. Suddenly, Williams had been cut off from those contacts which had always been the source of his creativity. Yet, by May he was already emphasizing the positive consequences of his setback in a letter to Louis Martz. "This is the second time I have been knocked out"—he had had a less serious stroke in 1948—"But this time I seem to have come out of it with a clearer head. Perhaps it derived from a feeling that I might have died, or, worse, have been left with a mind permanently incapacitated." Williams goes on to speak optimistically of the "opportunity for thought" and reading afforded by his new idleness. He had been reading a translation of Homer's *Iliad*, and this has enabled him "to 'place' the new in relation to the past much more accurately. . . . We have been looking for too big, too spectacular a divergence from the old. The 'new measure' is much more particular, much more related to the remote past than I, for one, believed. It was a natural blunder from the excess of our own feelings, but one that must now be corrected" and so, he declares, "we are through with the crude 'fight' we have had to wage. Our position is now established, the approach must be more an inversion upon ourselves . . . a thing we didn't have time for formerly." Williams chastizes himself for the failure to "make myself clear" and directs himself toward "a final summary" (*SL*, pp. 298–99).

The tone and substance of this letter reveal much about the mood in which Williams's later poems were written. Now willing to acknowledge continuities between his work and that of the past, Williams no longer conceives of himself as the combative revolutionary, cutting through the dried husks of dead forms in order to begin anew. That crude fight is over. In particular he now feels no need to contend against the pressure of historical time; it is as if, having come so close to death and having retired from the rushed life of a physician, Williams's life became a prolonged instant, completely outside the passage of time—an eternal moment. Williams had always sought to find the all in the momentary; but while the early work suggests the presence of the archetypal hidden in the instant, the last poems emphasize the eternal over the immediate and bring the universalizing process very much to the surface of the poetry. The poet turns increasingly inward, often into personal memory, an inversion upon himself made possible by the new leisurely pace of his life, and his manner becomes more obviously symbolic and even elegant. Williams's whole above-the-battle stance in the letter to Prof. Martz suggests the kind of eternal perspective from which the later poems are written, and it is a perspective which emphasizes unities rather than distinctions. The crude, earthy aspect of Williams's personality falls away; we see the emergence of a much more relaxed and sagacious figure, close to the humble and kindly spirit of St. Francis of Assisi Williams describes in "The Mental Hospital Garden." His illness and retirement brought a new season into Williams's life, and he met it by advancing an entirely new style of verse—a remarkable achievement for a man in his seventies.

It is in the context of this shift in Williams's position that we should approach *Paterson* V. The publication of this book, seven years after the apparent completion of the poem, revived the critical debate about the nature and even the existence of the poem's unity. Addition of the fifth book has been defended by several critics who cite Williams's belief in "open form." Walter Sutton argues,

> The addition of another part or an indefinite number of parts is in accord with Dr. Williams's theory of the poem. For to him the whole of *Paterson*, or of any poem, can be construed as a search for adequate form, a search that is always advancing, as it must advance, in time, but that is never completed.[2]

Prof. Sutton's article is an important early attempt to explore *Paterson's* form from the inside. Books I–IV do enact a process of creation and disintegration which *is* the poem's form, and the close of Book IV, its image of the explorer heading inland with his dog, is certainly an instance of the open ending: the image suggests a search that is continuing rather than finished. Presumably, further episodes, illustrating this never-ending quest from new angles of vision, could be added. The trouble with this line of argument is that while it could be used to justify the inclusion of a fifth or even an "indefinite number of parts," it does not quite apply to the fifth book we do have. For the Paterson of this book is not the kind of explorer we see at the end of Book IV. He is no longer struggling to get into the position in which to write; he now occupies that position. Instead of splitting things down to their elementary particles, his aim is now to pull them together, easily, into unity. In fact, it was clearly to incorporate this new perspective into his major work that Williams wrote Book V.

Hence Louis Martz comes much closer to the truth when he calls *Paterson* V "an epilogue or coda." [3] Its relation to Books I–IV is different from the relations of the original four books to each other. In his working notes for Book V Williams speaks of one incident as "the same as in Book II *but in a different key*"; [4] Book V is a coda in which the author reviews earlier episodes and motifs, their discordancies now resolved in a new mood of harmonious affirmation. In Book II Paterson walks up Garrett Mountain in a frustrating search for beauty; in Book V Audubon walks through the wilderness "across three states" to discover "a horned beast among the trees" (p. 245), the mythical unicorn which becomes the book's recurrent symbol for beauty. In Book III Paterson can only release his creative powers by purging his mind of the art of the past, but he can now speak of The Cloisters, the New York City museum where he saw a series of medieval tapestries describing the hunt of the unicorn, as "real" (p. 244); again, his crude fight with the past is over. At the end of Book I Paterson quotes John Addington Symond's defense of the Greeks' use of "deformed and mutilated verses" as appropriate to "the distorted subjects with which they dealt" (p. 53), the quote serving to justify the mutilated form of his own poem. But in Book V "all the deformities take wing" (p. 238) and Paterson translates a lyric by Sappho who, we are told, "wrote for a clear gentle tinkling voice. She avoided all roughness" (p. 253). In *Paterson* V the poet does not keep breaking through form to get at the substance; he celebrates the marriage of contemporary matter with eternal form.

The seven Unicorn Tapestries at The Cloisters serve Williams as both an instance of and a means to this kind of artistic unity. They combine painstaking devotion to detail with an awareness of archetypal pattern in a way that makes them an ideal union of the literal and the mythical.[5] Moreover, just as Williams now conceives of himself as part of a community of artists, rather than as the isolated rebel, the tapestries were woven by a group of men and women, young and old, "all together, working together" (p. 270); they define art as a collective enterprise. At one point Williams refers to the tapestries as a "living fiction" (p. 272), a paradox that self-consciously concedes their status as art works but still insists on their continuing vitality. In fact, this paradox also suggests how the tapestries can work as an organizing device in the poem itself: since they are recurrent, the same patterns we find there can be found in contemporary experience. In the middle ages the hunt of the unicorn was usually allegorized into the story of Christ, with the captured animal in the final tapestry standing for the resurrected saviour. In Williams's work, the unicorn stands for the artist or the imagination, their transcendence of time, suffering, and death: the beast in the final tapestry is wounded, penned in, but regal and indifferent and thus unconquerable. The unicorn becomes a more elegant and more universal symbol for that beauty Paterson had found in the girl in the basement in Book III. In these tapestries he finds a rich set of equivalents for his own quest, a symbolic legend that amplifies, elevates and pulls together the details of his own poem; they *are* a living fiction.

But it is important to see exactly the kind of unity Williams is after here. *Paterson* V is also broken into discrete blocks of material, individual parts are still kept separate; their joining occurs as an imaginative process, not as a static fusion. Instead

of creating, for example, a finished symbolic narrative, Williams gives us both the raw material and the symbolic tapestries—allowing their combination to occur as a process in the
mind of the reader. Modern and ancient, literal and symbolic,
wind in and out of the poem "contrapuntally" (p. 278), in an
imaginative dance. A look at a passage near the end of Part III
of Book V will show us how this process works in the poem.

>   —the aging body
>   with the deformed great-toe nail
> makes itself known
>   coming
>   to search me out—with a
>   rare smile
> among the thronging flowers of that field
>   where the Unicorn
>   is penned by a low
> wooden fence
>   in April!
>   the same month
> when at the foot of the post
>   he saw the man dig up
> the red snake and kill it with a spade
>   Godwin told me
>   its tail
> would not stop wriggling till
>   after the sun
>   goes down—
> he knew everything
>   or nothing
>   and died insane
> when he was still a young man   (pp. 270-71)

The passage begins with a backyard scene in the present,
equates it with a scene from the Unicorn Tapestries, then
shifts back from this metaphorization of experience to a specific memory of boyhood trauma. The three parts, placed side
by side in a loosely associative fashion, are kept discrete, their
relations left unstated, open. The reader is therefore asked to
circle around within this unit and discover, not a single unify-

ing idea, but a complex network of relations. One motif is the
sense of a tenacious holding onto life. There is the poet's wife
who, in spite of old age's deformities, still asserts a physical
presence (it is her body, not, say, her voice that makes her
known) as well as an undying love ("rare smile") for him.
There is Paterson himself who, unlike Godwin, has been
penned in by old age, the roles of husband and father, but
who, like the unicorn, has nevertheless maintained a kind of
sexual and imaginative potency. There is finally the tenacity of
the snake which, with its head crushed, wriggles violently until
sundown. Yet the emphasis in this last episode is less on persistence than on the place of death in the cycles of nature and on
Godwin's knowledge of these mysterious processes. In fact,
Godwin's wisdom is like the awareness of the artist who can
equate his domestic affairs with the symbolic patterns of a medieval tapestry; both are forms of knowing which, staying
close to physical experience, involve a sense of what is recurrent in such experience. And it is this sense that his own life is
simply one manifestation of an eternally recurrent pattern that
frees Paterson from all fear of death.

What is most striking about this passage to any reader of the
first four books of *Paterson* is its stress on the harmonies,
rather than the tensions, among its parts. The use of the poetic
fiction, the unicorn as analogue for the poet, would earlier have
been broken down ironically, but it here serves to amplify the
significance of the contemporary material. In the passage following the one we have just been looking at, Paterson turns
self-consciously around to meditate about the movement of his
own thoughts; but the result, again, is no reversal but an ex-
pansion of idea and mood.

        The (self) direction has been changed
                the serpent
                        its tail in its mouth
        "the river has returned to its beginnings"
                and backward
                        (and forward)
        it tortures itself within me

                         until time has been washed finally under:
                         and "I knew all (or enough)
    it became me   .   "
                         —the times are not heroic
    since then
                         but they are cleaner
                         and freer of disease
    the mind rotted within them   .
                         we'll say
                              the serpent
    has its tail in its mouth
                         AGAIN!
                         the all-wise serpent   (p. 271)

Paterson steps back to view his present situation in the context
of his entire career. In old age, he says, the self is forced to
take up new directions—specifically, those opened by personal
memory. The kind of reminiscence he is talking about, however, is not just an old man's mind drifting into random recollection. The snake with its tail in its mouth, the river returning
to its beginnings: both of these images remind us that the act
of memory, in its circularity, achieves a transcendence of time.
What is remembered is, after all, what has persisted through
time; and it has persisted because, like the memory of Godwin
that suddenly surfaces from the subconscious, it has an archetypal status. The quoted lines in the passage are taken from
"The Wanderer"; they serve as an instance as well as a definition of memory. Paterson, circling back from the end to the
beginning of his career, then bringing himself up to the present again, moves backward and forward so that time *is* finally
washed under. Old age may be less heroic, its tone is certainly
more modest, it entails a lessening of perceptual powers but,
through memory, "the serpent // has its tail in its mouth /
AGAIN!"; the process of renewal goes on.

    Most of the later poems share the impulse in *Paterson* V to
pull things together into this easygoing, circling process. Williams himself regarded the work of this period as the summit
of his art; and the general tendency among his critics has been
to echo this judgment.[6] Certainly the image the poems project

—a benevolent old man, recovering from some near fatal illness, now filled with love, blessing all he sees, humbly dispensing wisdom—is a touching one. Moreover, the changed circumstances of Williams's life resulted in a more personal and discursive medium while this very step back from immediate experience made possible a greater degree of artistic finish. All this has made the Williams of the 1950's a figure hard to resist; but our admiration for his tenacity in developing a new mode, our engagement with the figure in the poems, must be separated from our estimate of the poetry. For in his later years Williams more and more found himself irresistible and, his self-divisions resolved, lost much of his capacity for self-criticism. This is already evident in the *Autobiography* (1951) where Williams tries to persuade us of his essential innocence, honesty and tenderness and, in the process, tells us everything but how this simple, rustic figure could have produced the tough, involuted verse and prose of William Carlos Williams. In the more reminiscent of the poems there is a similar proclivity to project present equanimity onto the past. The new looseness of manner and tenderness of feeling can sometimes sink into the sort of soggy, uplifting didacticism that had prompted Imagism in the first place. At the very least, it seems to me an open question whether the divisions of Williams's character did not generate an intense, multi-dimensional language in *Spring and All* that makes that book superior to the works of the middle 'fifties. Williams, of course, continued to write some fine poems: "To Daphne and Virginia," "The Orchestra," "The Yellow Flower," "The Mental Hospital Garden," "The Desert Music," "The Pink Locust," "Shadows" and "Asphodel, That Greeny Flower." [7] But even among these, the best tend to be the more self-conscious, notably the "Asphodel" poem.

"Asphodel, That Greeny Flower" is a rather long meditative poem, divided into three books and a coda. The poet is addressing his wife, whom he has abused through his sexual and artistic pursuits. He is approaching her one last time, reviewing their life together and asking her forgiveness. Here Williams is

no longer dispersing himself into a set of objects; the "I,"
slowly purged from his verse in the teens, now returns in the
figure of a wise old man who, while aware of loss and suffering, offers advice, hope and consolation. Old age has always
held its right to its opinions and Williams is now not reluctant
to state his explicitly.

> So we come to watch time's flight
> as we might watch
> summer lightning
> or fireflies, secure
> by grace of the imagination,
> safe in its care.   (pp. 179–80)

Time is finally powerless to affect us, Williams tells us in a
voice of grandfatherly solicitude. Yet, he can also discourse
somberly, and again explicitly, about its effects on our physical
powers.

> Approaching death
> as we think, the death of love,
> no distinction
> any more suffices to differentiate
> the particulars
> of place and condition
> with which we have been long
> familiar.   (p. 162)

The outlines of things are not so distinct any more. And so,
instead of cutting things down to "isolate flecks" and juxtapos-
ing them in empty space, he supplies many transitional links,
fills in the spaces between images.

> The sea! The sea!
> Always
> when I think of the sea
> there comes to mind
> the *Iliad*
> and Helen's public fault
> that bred it.   (p. 158)

Not all transitions are made so explicitly, but even when they
are not, the shifts are never violent; there is never the tension

of opposed forces that we find in *Spring and All*. Moreover, in "Asphodel" Williams often explains the significances of his images. After describing "the statue / of Colleoni's horse / with the thickset little man // on top / in armor / presenting a naked sword" and "the horse rampant / roused by the mare in / the Venus and Adonis," Williams comments that "these are pictures / of crude force" (p. 171). "Of love, abiding love // it will be telling," he says of the asphodel (p. 153). As we shall see, the images in this poem are rich, fluid, complex; his comments by no means exhaust their significance. But the effect of this discursive quality is to ease the reader's movement through the verse. "It is not // a flute note either, it is the relation / of a flute note / to a drum," Williams writes in "The Orchestra" (*PB*, p. 81). Relations here emerge as more important than discrete objects, and these relations are often articulated at the surface of the poetry. Creative activity now takes place at a "higher" level of consciousness; Williams does not take us to the edge of unconscious chaos but to a place in the mind where form and continuity become more predominant.

Williams's poetry of the 1950's thus has a more accessible surface—a fact that accounts for its greater critical popularity. Other manifestations of this loosening up are his unequivocal acceptance of romantic feeling and his dependence on personal, biographical material. In "Asphodel," emotions, like ideas, are often stated: "with fear in my heart" (p. 154), "I regret" (p. 169), "I adore" (p. 169), "I am tortured // and cannot rest" (p. 170). Moreover, these feelings are much tenderer than any Williams had previously been willing to admit to his verse; emotion ranges from "every drill / driven into the earth // for oil enters my side / also" (p. 168) through "our eyes fill / with tears" (p. 153) to "Sweet, creep into my arms!" (p. 175). He is embarrassed neither by uplifting sentiments—"the palm goes // always to the light" (p. 180)—nor by poignancy:

> At the altar
> so intent was I
> before my vows
> so moved by your presence
> a girl so pale

> and ready to faint
>   that I pitied
>   and wanted to protect you. (p. 181)

A sad, tender, consoling mood is evoked, one that is never violently undercut by a tougher voice uttering "pah!" or "pinholes" or the like. The mood *is* complex, including the torture of oil drills as well as the celebration of the light; but whereas in *Spring and All* light and darkness were left in a kind of agonizing tension, we now get a resolution of conflict: "the palm goes // always to the light."

The quality of the feeling stems, of course, from the poem's origin in a specific personal situation: Williams's ambivalent relation with his wife, Flossie. In *The Build-up*, the last novel in the *White Mule* trilogy, Williams describes his rather peculiar courtship of Flossie. He proposed to her, it appears, a few days after her older sister, with whom he was in love, was engaged to his younger brother. He defines the love between them as "not romantic love" but "a dark sort of passion . . . a passion of despair, as all life is despair" (p. 262). He is evading a good deal here, but the feeling he speaks of—an acceptance of what imperfectly exists—is exactly that dark passion we have seen animating all of his creative work; Flossie is its ultimate source. But even if she was "the rock on which I have built" (*Auto*, p. 55), Williams frequently wandered off. In the *Autobiography* she remains a rather dim figure, given a few vague tributes, but essentially in the background; and in some respects that must have seemed to her her place in his life. Medicine, poetry, and other women occupied much more of his time than domestic pursuits. As early as the "Prologue" to *Kora in Hell*, Williams had argued that love, like literary style, had periodically to be broken down in order to come to new life (*SE*, p. 20). Love had to be constantly reborn out of its own despair. Yet it would be surprising if Flossie did not occasionally feel that her husband's affairs were more a form of self-indulgence than a rather strange way of renewing their marriage; and being the ultimate source of the poet's work is a fairly abstract role for his wife to adopt. The tensions that developed in their marriage were first explored in Williams's best play, *A Dream of Love* (1948)—and they provide the background for "Asphodel."

In the poem, Williams now turns to address his wife directly and remorsefully. Old, nearing death, he approaches her "perhaps for the last time" (p. 154). The time is winter, but this is more an internal state than a season in Rutherford—defined by the strong sense of loss, fading, and mutability with which the poem begins. "Today // I'm filled with the fading memory of those flowers / that we both loved," Williams says (p. 153). He recalls first the "poor // colorless" (p. 153) asphodel, a flower that grows in the meadows of New Jersey, but also (he had read in Homer) along the fields in the underworld. In fact, Williams speaks at the start as if from among the dead, identifying with their groping recollection as they gaze at the asphodel: "What do I remember / that was shaped / as this thing is shaped?" (p. 153). "There is something / something urgent" (p. 154) which he *must* say, but he does not want to rush it—"while I drink in / the joy of your approach, / perhaps for the last time" (p. 154)—and fading powers of memory make it hard to begin. There is an urgency about the very act of speech: "I dare not stop. / Listen while I talk on // against time." "Only give me time," he asks,

> time to recall them
> before I shall speak out
Give me time,
> time.   (p. 154)

He gropes for memory, for speech, for his wife's love—the three will become identified in the course of the poem—for these have the power to save him from time's push toward oblivion; they can bring him back from the realm of the dead.

At the end of Book III of "Asphodel" Williams does gain the forgiveness he seeks: "You have forgiven me / making me new again" (p. 177). And the asphodel becomes the appropriate symbol for this renewal of love in the poet's old age: though colorless and odorless, "little prized among the living"

(p. 153), it is a sturdy perennial: "I have invoked the flower /
in that // frail as it is / after winter's harshness / it comes
again" (pp. 169–70). The basic pattern of "Asphodel," the
transition from death to life, is a familiar one in Williams's
work. But one important difference from the earlier treatment
of this process is the change in the length and pace of the
poem—that is, in the poet's sense of time. The poem is strongly
reminiscent, but it is located in a now: the line breaks give the
isolated word "today" equal weight with "I'm filled with the
fading memory of those flowers." Memory soon begins to
flow, but Williams keeps turning back from recollection of
their long life together to their present situation. "Inseparable
from the fire / its light / takes precedence over it," Williams
writes in the Coda.

> In the huge gap
>   between the flash
> and the thunderstroke
>   spring has come in
>   or a deep snow fallen.
> Call it old age.
>   In that stretch
>   we have lived to see
> a colt kick up his heels.
>   Do not hasten
>   laugh and play
> in an eternity
>   the heat will not overtake the light.
>   (pp. 178–79)

The urgency felt at the start of the poem has vanished. Precedence of the light over the fire guarantees that death is not,
as we think, the death of love. Old age need not be merely an
experience of loss and emptiness. If youth can be filled with a
multiplicity of physical sensations, old age can achieve a full-
ness of the imagination. In fact, variants of the word "fill"
echo and re-echo through this poem. The life of the poet and
his wife has been "filled" with flowers, their eyes "fill" with

tears, Williams's mind is now "filled" with the fading memory of those flowers. At one point speech almost lapses into silence, emptiness.

> Silence can be complex too,
> > but you do not get far
> > > with silence.
> Begin again.
> > It is like Homer's
> > > catalogue of ships:
> it fills up the time.   (p. 159)

Context, aided by the isolation of the phrase in its own line, gives a cynical slang expression ("well, it fills up the time") a poetic and a more positive force. Silence is emptiness, death; speech makes the time full, and this is one of the ways in which poetic speech and love are identified. "Do not hasten / laugh and play // in an eternity." At the brink of death, in that instant between the flash and the thunderstroke, Williams opens a "huge gap" and fills it with the unhurried recollections and discursive wisdom of this poem. The suspended moment he had always sought is now stretched out, expanded into "an eternity"; the heat will not overtake the light.

This sense of the eternal moment, however, importantly qualifies any sense in which the poem can be called personal. The "I" is there, and the events of the speaker's life are clearly those of Williams's. Yet, the stress here is on the metaphorization of experience; the author sees his life as a living fiction. Past events are frequently rendered figuratively. The time of youthful passion is a "garden" (p. 156), while the later trials of marriage are a "storm" (p. 157). Williams compares his own leisurely manner of discourse with "Homer's / catalogue of ships," then takes a step back to comment on his technique.

> I speak in figures,
> > well enough, the dresses
> you wear are figures also,
> > we could not meet
> > > otherwise.   (p. 159)

Emphasis has shifted from a kind of naked utterance—the bare object—to a more figurative style, and the figures themselves—like the comparison between metaphor and clothing—are deliberately more conventional than startling. All of the poem's central metaphors—flower, garden, sea, storm, fire, light—are commonplace in literature. What is more, they are not given any novel twist, of the sort spring receives in "By the road," to give them the fresh impact of literal experience.

Even more important than their commonplace quality is the way the figures work in this poem. In *Spring and All* Williams pushed away from conventional symbolism, down into the literal, there to discover a new symbolic world. But in "Asphodel," his main tendency is to move through the literal toward the symbolic, though he is self-conscious about speaking in figures and keeps coming back to the literal to verify his hardmindedness. In Book III Williams recalls "waiting at a station / with a friend," "a distinguished artist," when "a fast freight / thundered through." "That's what we'd all like to be, Bill," the friend commented—showing exactly that sense of the all in the momentary that made him a distinguished artist (p. 171). Throughout "Asphodel" Williams himself keeps discovering the archetypal in the particular. Just after the episode with his artist friend, Williams recalls a man seen "yesterday / in the subway." A detailed account of the man's mixture of crudity and refinement follows; then Williams suddenly realizes why he is so intrigued by this person.

>   This man
>   reminds me of my father.
> I am looking
>   into my father's
>   face!

The image of the man expands still further; he becomes the universal father: "With him // went all men / and all women too / were in his loins."

>   And so, by chance,
>   how should it be otherwise?

> from what came to me
>
> in a subway train
>
> I build a picture
>
> of all men. (pp. 172–74)

It is memory that, re-awakened, enables the older poet to transcend time: as he moves back, first through personal and then
the racial past, he gets to the eternal, the archetypal. Moreover, mythic vision has not been dispersed into scattered details in the verse, to be perceived in sudden flashes; the process
of its recovery has been brought up to the surface of the poetry.

This universalizing process is going on constantly in "Asphodel." The speaker may be the particular person "Bill" Williams, but he is also the (timeless) father of all poets,
Homer—with strong suggestions of his difference from the
weary, death-longing Tiresias of "The Waste Land."

> Death is no answer,
>
> no answer—
>
> to a blind old man
>
> whose bones
>
> have the movement
>
> of the sea,
>
> a sexless old man
>
> for whom it is a sea
>
> of which his verses
>
> are made up. (p. 166)

Williams is highly self-conscious about this kind of poetic
speech, and his tentativeness makes it easier for the reader to
accept the process of metaphorization. "Fanciful or not," he
says of his thoughts about the old man in the subway (p. 174).
At the very beginning of the poem he is hesitant about asserting a metaphor too boldly:

> We lived long together
>
> a life filled,
>
> *if you will,*
>
> with flowers. [my emphasis] (p. 153)

He is aware that his reader is apt to take "lightly" what is said in poems, that poems in his world are "despised poems" (p. 161). He has to turn around on, and gently defend, himself: "I speak in figures." All of this helps to define the speaker as one who is not blindly, arrogantly, pushing experience into forms, unities. The poem does not simply proclaim a synthesis—it gives us a process, a process in which images are constantly expanding toward the archetypical, contracting to the literal, expanding again, and so on. This process can best be seen in Williams's handling of the figure of Flossie.

It is important to see that, while Williams is sorry for the pain he has caused his wife, he does not try to revoke his past life. "I do not come to you / abjectly // with confessions of my faults" (p. 170). Instead, he tries to "give the steps" "by which you shall mount, / again to think well of me" (p. 171). Her forgiveness is to come from her understanding of the peculiar nature of his love for her. From the first, the love she awoke in him was expansive, all-embracing:

> Endless wealth,
>   I thought,
>   held out its arms to me.
> A thousand topics
>   in an apple blossom.
>   The generous earth itself
> gave us lief.
>   The whole world
>   became my garden! (pp. 155–56)

Accordingly, Flossie is not just Flossie; she is a "single image" running through all things (p. 169). This figure freed Williams to pluck many other flowers of the field and created some of the main tensions of their marriage. Williams knows that this argument will not seem "wholly credible" (p. 154), but he insists that love should not be a limiting thing:

>   Love is something else,
>   or so I thought it,
> a garden which expands,
>   though I knew you as a woman

                        and never thought otherwise,
        until the whole sea
                has been taken up
                        and all its gardens. (p. 160)

Love at first vaguely expands, then turns back to the literal
"you," then reaches out toward the all, the whole sea. In the
following lines Williams fills in our sense of the all, but comes
back again at the end to the "you" which is love's source.

    It was the love of love
                the love that swallows up all else
                        a grateful love,
        a love of nature, of people
                animals,
                        a love engendering
        gentleness and goodness
                that moved me
                        and *that* I saw in you. (p. 160).

Shifts of direction like this have always been characteristic of
Williams's work, though they are now less rapid and startling.
Their importance here, however, is that they enact the notion
of love as a force that expands to the all, then returns to its origin, in the movement of the verse; in the poem Flossie *is* the
single image that generates all the others.

    Near the end of Book III, after he has invoked some of the
flowers that counted most for them, Williams says,

    You were like those,
                though I quickly
                        correct myself
        for you were a woman
                and no flower
                        and had to face
        the problems which confront a woman.
                But you were for all that
                        flowerlike
        and I say this to you now
                and it is a thing
                        which compounded

> my torment
>> that I never
>>> forgot it.   (p. 177)

Again, the poet self-consciously asserts, takes back, then reasserts a poetic figure. And when the comparison is finally made, it is stated carefully—as a simile. Williams had once declared that "the coining of similes is a pastime of very low order" (*SE*, p. 16); but explicit comparisons frequently enter his later poetry. They are ideally suited for creating the kind of loose unity Williams was after in these poems: they establish a relation between, but not a fusion of, the two items compared. Flossie is "a woman" and "no flower"; but she is also "flower-*like*" [my emphasis].

The literal presence of Flossie is extremely important; she is the "rock" on which the rest of the poem is built. As in *Spring and All* and *Paterson*, Williams creates a poetic field by means of recurrent words, images. Crucial figures in "Asphodel" are the flower, garden, sea. At the very beginning asphodel, "that greeny flower," is formally announced as the poetic subject. The poet reflects on a "long" life "filled" "with flowers" and is thus "cheered" "to know / that there were flowers also / in hell" (p. 153). Book I is filled with flowers. There are a variety of specific flowers, memories of youthful passion: buttercup, honeysuckle, lily, rose hedges, pink mallow, orchid, lilies-of-the-valley; the word "flower(s)" appears fourteen times. Yet images in this poem quickly move toward the symbolic. When Williams tells us that the "storm" "is a flower" (p. 157), we read "marital turbulence" for storm and "love" for flower. Similarly, when he uses the word "garden," he is not pointing toward "this garden," he is invoking the *idea* of gardens. But those equivalences are not static; for the way the recurrences in this poem work is to take a traditional literary figure—like the garden—and make it more open, fluid, expansive. In its multiplicity the flower becomes a garden; with the awakening of his love for Flossie, says Williams, "The whole world / became my garden!" At this point the writer, as if questioning his hyperbole, self-consciously interrupts himself and remembers the garden's opposite: "But the sea / which no one tends. . . ." Yet this turn—in a manner characteristic of this poem—does not undercut the garden image but extends it:

> But the sea
>   which no one tends
>   is also a garden

The thought does not stop here, however; the comparison is qualified: the sea is a garden "when the sun strikes it / and the waves / are wakened." At such moments "it puts all flowers / to shame." Yet, from this affirmation of the sea's beauty, Williams can turn around to concede its death and ugliness:

>   Too, there are the starfish
>   stiffened by the sun
>   and other sea wrack
>   and weeds.   (p. 156)

The sea is a garden; the sea is not a garden. As in *Paterson*, the sea is recognized as death; but "the sea alone // with its multiplicity / holds any hope" (p. 158). Niggardliness, the fear of that "love that swallows up all else" (p. 160), the single-minded thrust through the world, ends in death, silence, despair—a desert. But surrender to multiplicity—as with the old man "whose bones // have the movement / of the sea," "for whom it is a sea / of which his verses / are made up" (p. 166)—cures "the mind" and "the will becomes again / a garden" (p. 159). The way Williams keeps turning back before going on, but keeps moving forward, defines the similarity to and difference from his earlier work. The motion of this poem is through a recognition of the fact of death, toward an affirmation of the transcendent power of love—symbolized by the asphodel, the flower that grows "in hell." This circling movement keeps going throughout the poem, through the elaborate dissection of "the deaths I suffered" (p. 164) in Book II, to culminate in the affirmations at the end of III:

>   Don't think
>   that because I say this

                    in a poem
                            it can be treated lightly
        or that the facts will not uphold it.
                    Are facts not flowers
                            and flowers facts
        or poems flowers
                    or all works of the imagination
                            interchangeable?
        Which proves
                    that love
                            rules them all, for then
        you will be my queen,
                    my queen of love
                            forever more.   (p. 178)

At this climactic point the poet's self-conscious awareness of
the frivolousness that most men associate with figurative
speech is absorbed into a firm instructional tone, "Don't think"
—while his own counter-assertion of the identity of fact and
figure is made gently, as a rhetorical question. Earlier, Williams had spoken of "the free interchange // of light" on the
sea's surface (p. 165). All things are works of the imagination,
and they are all interchangeable—like the images of this poem
—because they are all manifestations of a single principle, the
light. These things are not fused; but they are joined. It was
this all-pervading light that "was wakened / and shone" at
"our wedding" (p. 181). Whether we accept Williams's argument of a "single image" running through the multiplicity of
his loves as credible or not, the important point is that his argument is made good in the structure of his poem. The way its
images split and join, split and join—their fluidity and openness
—shows that love does rule them all.
    "Asphodel" is written in the triadic stanza pattern which,
taken over from the "descent beckons" passage in *Paterson* II,
Williams employed in all but one of the poems in *The Desert
Music* and *Journey to Love*. In theorizing about the poem
Williams always dwelt on its basic structural unit—the line.
The iambic pentameter line, or any line measured by counting
stresses or syllables, seemed to him too rigid to express the
modern sense of reality. Poems, he argues,

cannot any longer be made following a Euclidian measure, "beautiful" as this may make them. The very grounds for our beliefs have altered. We do not live that way any more; nothing in our lives, at bottom, is ordered according to that measure; our social concepts, our schools, our very religious ideas, certainly our understanding of mathematics are greatly altered. . . . Only the construction of our poems—and at best the construction of a poem must engage the tips of our intellectual awareness—is left shamefully to the past. (*SE,* p. 337)

At the same time Williams was just as opposed to free verse as he was to more archaic ways of ordering. If the second pushes down too hard from the outside, the first lifts not at all and creates no tension in the poem; both, by blurring experience, fail to bring its distinct elements into the kind of proximity that will create an imaginative field. Only invention can do that; "poetry is creation of new form—" (*SL,* p. 134); and the rhythmical sources of that form will be found not in the literature of the past but in the spoken language of today, the American idiom. Hence, what Williams was after was a new way of measuring, one more consonant with the speech, with the realities of our time. As he told Kay Boyle in 1932, this new measure "must be large enough, free enough, elastic enough, new enough yet firm enough to hold the new well, without spilling. It must have a form" (*SL,* p. 133). How to uncover this new form? "Relativity gives us the cue," says Williams, directing us to a "*relatively* stable foot, not a rigid one" (*SE,* p. 340). His lifelong search for such a new measure culminated, he believed, in the triadic stanza, its use of a "variable foot."

A relative stability? A variable foot? Williams is well aware that these phrases will strike a certain kind of mind as contradictory; he is trying to dissolve what he takes to be a false antithesis in such minds. The real question is, what do these notions mean when applied to a specific passage of verse? In public discussions of this new measure Williams stays tantalizingly abstract, abundant on theory but wary of examples. But in a letter to Richard Eberhart he reveals that "by measure I mean musical pace" and that he counts one for each of the three feet in a stanza (*SL*, pp. 326–27). The practice, it appears, is rather easily understood and much less radical than the theory would lead us to expect: uniform intervals of lapsed time (musical pace) establish a regularity in the poem; but the syllable count, ranging from one to thirteen in "Asphodel," is variable, with pauses used to fill out the intervals in the shorter lines. Whether or not this line will, as Williams believed, open the way for poets to come, only the future can tell. But it is perfectly suited to the mood and point of view of the poems of his own old age.

In the triadic stanza, the line begins to move across the page, turns slightly back, begins again, goes through another short turn, then begins once more—before turning all the way back to the left hand margin. The medium itself suggests the kind of halting progression, self-conscious affirmation, that we find in a poem like "Asphodel." This quality can be best epitomized by a passage in which Williams simultaneously quotes Spenser's "Prothalamion" and alludes to "The Waste Land."

> All pomp and ceremony
>   of weddings,
> "Sweet Thames, run softly
>   till I end
>   my song,"—
> are of an equal sort.   (p. 181)

Williams's three-stepped stanza does take away much of the flow of Spenser's line. But while in Eliot's shattered world this mellifluousness can only be used ironically, Williams's breaking of the line does not undercut—it prolongs, deepens, extends; it makes possible a tentative acceptance of the whole mood and manner implied by Spenser's line. Williams is still spacing things out carefully, isolating them in rather short lines; but he now does this much more gently and builds a halting but genuine rhythmic flow. The lines, while momentarily suspended as individual units, do move across the page in a fairly regular pattern: if there is not the flow possible in a line of iambic pentameter, there is not the tensed, jagged quality of Wil-

liams's earlier work either. "Asphodel" has more the ease of a
matured craftsmanship.

The freedom of the "variable foot" still requires its own
kind of discipline: since the syllable count is variable, each line
break must still carry its own justification. Hence, in spite of
the regular pace, each line must be filled subtly, attentively.
To begin with, the line divisions (as always in Williams) slow
down movement of the verse, momentarily isolate syntactic
units—giving each an interval of its own, time to sink into the
mind. Under Williams's careful hand, parts we might otherwise glide past are given emphatic weight and more exact
meaning. There is a delicate but significant difference between
this line from "Asphodel"

> The end
> > will come
> > > in its time.   (p. 165)

and these two of many possible variants:

> The end will come in its time.

> > > The end will come
> in its time.

The first variant rushes, as if eager to dismiss thoughts of the
end; the second, by cutting the sentence across a stanza break,
stresses that the end will come *when it comes*. Williams's version, descending deliberately across the page, gives equal stress
to "end," "come" and "time" and is thus the only one of the
three which defines a full and measured acceptance of death
over which we have no control.

Similarly, at the beginning of the "Coda" Williams writes,

> Inseparable from the fire,
> > its light
> > > takes percedence over it.

Light takes precedence not just by assertion of the poet but by
its fulfillment of syntactic expectations raised by "inseparable,"

its short, closed sound, its near isolation in a line that is surrounded by longer, quicker lines. Williams goes on:

> Then follows
> > what we have dreaded—
> > but it can never
> overcome what has gone before.   (p. 178)

"Then follows" puts us into the dimension of temporal sequence; we wait, expectantly, for what follows to be named.
Instead, the next line tells us more about our attitude (dread)
toward that thing than what that thing actually is. The dash at
the end of the line suggests that the object of dread may be
named in the following one, but the speaker turns away from
direct confrontation, toward assurance: "but it can never //
overcome what has gone before." Dividing auxiliary from
main verb across a stanza break gives great weight to both
"never" and "overcome." Both of these are time words—although "overcome," like "precedence," has connotations of
value too—and the turn back across the page shifts us out of
time as a forward-moving, irretrievable progression, and into
the eternal moment. An experience of the "light" does not
fade into the past and die; it is an experience of eternity and
stays alive forever—like the memory of his own wedding
which, Williams says at the end of the "Coda," has the power
to revive him *now*. This groping turn through the temporal
and into the eternal—typical of the entire poem—could not be
rendered in any other but the verse form Williams has employed.

The opening passage of the "Coda" shows that Williams still
suspends a grammatical expectation across a line or stanza division as a means of distributing emphasis exactly. But these divisions are much less striking than in *Spring and All*. Williams
will cut a line between subject and verb, verb and object, main
clause and subordinate clause, parts of a compound sentence.
He will even let "logic" words such as "and so" or "but if"
stand alone in a line. But he does not end lines strikingly with
prepositions, articles or (for the most part) adjectives. There is

less antagonism towards the conventional units of syntax, a fact also evident in the elimination of sentence fragments. Even more important, our expectations are not dealt with so violently: "what we have dreaded" may not be exactly what we anticipated, but it is not a reversal either. At the start of Book III Williams writes,

>   What power has love but forgiveness?
>   In other words
>   by its intervention
>   what has been done
>   can be undone.   (p. 169)

Argument has been distributed easily across these stanzas: lines mark off a sentence, a phrase, a phrase, a subject-clause, a verb. Reversal *is* the idea advanced—the denial of time via love—but the last line comes as the unraveling of a logical consequence of what has been stated in the first line. There is more the sense of a deliberate building toward a triumphant climax than the experience of a series of swift, startling turns of thought.

In "Asphodel" relations are more defined; ambiguities are cleaned away. Argument does not proceed remorselessly forward in a straight line; it circles, winds into progression, but its turning has been spread out more—like the lines across the page—making movement easier, more relaxed. Occasionally punctuation has been omitted to create alternate readings:

>   Do not hasten
>   laugh and play
>   in an eternity
>   the heat will not overtake the light.
>   (p. 179)

"In an eternity" can either go with what comes before ("laugh and play // in an eternity") or with what follows ("in an eternity / the heat will not overtake the light"). But the two senses work to fill out, amplify—not contradict—each other. As before, line breaks serve to point up turns in the thought. But now directions are not abruptly established by a shift of tone; they are eased by use of such logic words as "but,"

"save" and the like. Williams is especially given to shifting the
direction of thought across the long turn from the third line
of one stanza to the first line of the next. He does this twice in
the concluding passage of "Asphodel":

> As I think of it now,
>   after a lifetime,
>   it is as if
> a sweet-scented flower
>   were poised
>   and for me did open.
> Asphodel
>   has no odor
>   save to the imagination
> but it too
>   celebrates the light.
>   It is late
> but an odor
>   as from our wedding
>   has revived for me
> and begun again to penetrate
>   into all crevices
>   of my world.   (p. 182)

At first Williams expresses a strong sense of loss through the
passage of time. The old man modestly asserts a common-place
figure—the bride seemed "as if" a "sweet-scented flower"—but
the distance between "now" and then ("did open") is stressed.
The flower of old age, the asphodel, "has no odor"; and "it is
late." Yet each time Williams falls into this feeling of loss, the
imagination delivers an upward turn—one that occurs as the
lines move back across the page to the left margin: "but it
too," "but an odor." A strong line begins the final stanza too:
"and begun again to penetrate." At this point the imagination
has dissolved temporal progression; the imaginary odor has
begun *now* to fill *all* the dark and empty spaces of the poet's
world.

Another aspect of Williams's relaxed craftsmanship in this
poem is his willingness to draw on iambic rhythms as a technical resource.

Of asphodel, that greeny flower,
          like a buttercup
                    upon its branching stem
save that it's green and wooden—
          I come, my sweet,
                    to sing to you,   (p. 153)

the poem begins. Syllabic count ranges from four to nine in
these lines; but a strong iambic beat has been established by the
third line. Then, as Williams pulls back across the page to start
a new stanza, as he pulls back from the simile to give the literal
truth of the asphodel as well, a trochaic (reverse) beat is introduced. Then, with the asphodel established as both fact and
figure, Williams tightens into a regular two foot iambic beat
and the invocation comes to a formal close.

Iambic meter, inverted word order, poetic epithet and peri-
odic sentence structure all contribute to create a stylistic eleva-
tion. This is partly the deliberate heightening of a formal beginning; but it is not as atypical as we might at first suppose.
Williams has probably confused more readers than he has
helped by suggesting that these later poems employ the
"American idiom," the speech we hear spoken about us every
day. It is exceedingly difficult to establish norms that enable us
to distinguish spoken use of the language from other uses. But
it becomes pretty clear, when we write some of his sentences
out as prose, that Williams's utterance is more elevated than
common speech.

> Begin again. It is like Homer's catalogue of ships: it fills up
> the time. I speak in figures, well enough, the dresses you wear
> are figures also, we could not meet otherwise. When I speak
> of flowers it is to recall that at one time we were young. All
> women are not Helen, I know that, but have Helen in their
> hearts. My sweet, you have it also, therefore I love you and
> could not love you otherwise. (p. 159)

The personal pronouns "I" and "you," direct address to "my
sweet," an interrupter like "I know that," create a conversational tone. Accordingly, the diction stays simple, containing
only two words of more than two syllables. There *is* a flat,

loose, prosaic quality to the style, but no one in Rutherford ever spoke sentences like these. The passage, for one thing, has a slight incantatory effect. The words "time," "figures," "otherwise," "speak," "flowers," "Helen," "also," "love" are all repeated; some of these, along with "meet" and "sweet" and "know," have appeared several times earlier in the poem. In fact, not only are these sentences unlike natural speech, but the self-conscious use of poetic figures and the subdued incantation suggest that the intended effect is one of deliberate rather than spontaneous utterance. Rather than simply recording American speech, Williams's style operates at a level where a flat, discursive, conversational language has been gently pushed, one step upward, toward ritual expression. Like the asphodel, this style is mainly colorless, abstract; but it too celebrates the light and it does so in a way that has both ease *and* a formal elegance.

As a result, the style embodies that value of decorum which the poet argues for; we could not meet him otherwise. Formality, ritual, decorum—all these were values that the younger Williams had heaped contempt on. Now, that crude fight is over. In "Asphodel" Williams can quote Spenser, identify with Homer, use the language of courtly love, speak of the "*grace* of the imagination" (p. 180; my emphasis), extol "medieval pageantry," "the reading of Chaucer," a priest's (or a savage chieftain's) "raiment," celebrate "all the pomp and ceremony / of weddings" (p. 181). *All* are works of the imagination. Like his own poetic figures, these are all manifestations of that "single image," first opened by Flossie, to which, he now says, he had devoted his entire life. His earlier work had put us at that edge of consciousness where light becomes darkness, and darkness light. At the end, in "Asphodel," "it is all // a celebration of the light" (p. 181).

Notes

Most of the references to Williams's work have been made in my text. But in order to keep the text as clean as possible, I have given no specific references when the work is short (a lyric poem or short story) and the title is mentioned. In addition, where a single work is dealt with extensively, I give page numbers without repeating the title. The following abbreviations are used:

Poems (Rutherford, N.J.: privately printed, 1909)	*Poems*
Kora in Hell: Improvisations (San Francisco: City Lights, 1957)	*Kora*
Spring and All (Dijon: Contact, 1923)	*SA*
The Great American Novel (Paris: Contact, 1923)	*GAN*
In the American Grain (Norfolk, Conn.: New Directions, 1956)	*IAG*
A Voyage to Pagany (New York: The Macaulay Co., 1928)	*A Voyage*
A Novelette and Other Prose, 1921–31 (Toulon: TO, Publishers, 1932)	*A Novelette*
White Mule (Norfolk, Conn.: New Directions, 1938)	*WM*
In the Money (Norfolk, Conn.: New Directions, 1940)	*IM*
The Collected Earlier Poems (Norfolk, Conn.: New Directions, 1951)	*CEP*
The Autobiography of William Carlos Williams (New York: Random House, 1951)	*Auto*
Selected Essays (New York: Random House, 1954)	*SE*
Selected Letters, ed. John C. Thirlwall (New York: McDowell Obolensky, 1957)	*SL*

I Wanted To Write a Poem, ed. Edith Heal (Bos-   IW
  ton: Beacon Press, 1958)
The Farmers' Daughters: The Collected Stories of   FD
  William Carlos Williams (Norfolk, Conn.: New
  Directions, 1961)
Pictures from Brueghel and Other Poems (Norfolk,   PB
  Conn.: New Directions, 1962)
The Collected Later Poems (Norfolk, Conn.: New   CLP
  Directions, 1963)
Paterson (Norfolk, Conn.: New Directions, 1963)   P

CHAPTER I

1. Water Sutton, "A Visit with William Carlos Williams," *The Minnesota Review,* I (April 1961), 312.

2. See Erik Erikson's *Young Man Luther* (New York, 1958).

3. There is an excellent study of the relations between medicine and art in Williams by Kenneth Burke, "William Carlos Williams, 1883–1963," in *Language as Symbolic Action* (Berkeley and Los Angeles, 1966), pp. 282–91.

4. *The Letters of Ezra Pound, 1907–1941,* ed. D. D. Paige (New York, 1950), p. 8.

5. "America, Whitman, and the Art of Poetry," *The Poetry Journal* (November 1917), 31.

6. "An Essay on *Leaves of Grass*" first appeared in *Leaves of Grass: One Hundred Years After,* ed. Milton Hindus (Stanford, 1955), pp. 22–31.

7. Walter Sutton, "A Visit with William Carlos Willams," 312.

8. William Carlos Williams, "An Approach to the Poem," *English Institute Essays* (New York, 1948), pp. 67–68.

9. J. Hillis Miller, *Poets of Reality* (Cambridge, Mass., 1965), p. 288. Later on, discussing the descent/ascent pattern in Williams's work (pp. 336–39), Professor Miller himself implies that there is a kind of subject-object tension in Williams's work; but he does not relate these perceptions to his main thesis.

CHAPTER II

1. Henry Adams, *The Life of George Cabot Lodge,* in *The Shock of Recognition,* ed. Edmund Wilson (New York, 1955), p. 751.

2. Walt Whitman, "In Paths Untrodden," *Complete Poetry and Selected Prose*, ed. James E. Miller, Jr. (Boston, 1959), p. 84.

3. This theme is developed at length in Larzer Ziff, *The American 1890s* (New York, 1966).

4. Ezra Pound, *Gaudier-Brzeska, A Memoir* (Norfolk, Conn., 1960), p. 102.

5. Quoted in Robert Buttel, *Wallace Stevens, The Making of Harmonium* (Princeton, N.J., 1967), p. 47.

6. Such is the main thesis of Pound's *Patria Mia* (Chicago, 1960).

7. "Rebellion in Art," in *America in Crisis*, ed. Daniel Aaron (New York, 1952), pp. 205–6.

8. Unpublished letter in the poetry collection at the Lockwood Memorial Library, State University of New York at Buffalo.

9. An unpublished letter to Horace Gregory, May 9, 1944, in the Beinecke Library, Yale University, gives an account by Williams of a performance by Miss Graham; the biography project is mentioned in *SL*, p. 171.

10. William Carlos Williams, "An Essay on *Leaves of Grass*," 23.

11. Quoted in Constance Rourke, *Charles Sheeler* (New York, 1938), p. 49.

12. The subject of Williams's relation to modern painting has been perceptively explored by Abraham Jan Dijkstra, in "William Carlos Williams and Painting: The Hieroglyphics of a New Speech," unpublished dissertation (University of California, Berkeley, 1967).

13. *The New Age*, X (Feb. 15, 1912), 370.

14. George Santayana, *Winds of Doctrine* (New York, 1913), pp. 1–24. Subsequent references are made in the text.

15. T. E. Hulme, *Speculations* (New York, 1924), p. 97.

16. Ibid. p. 101.

17. T. E. Hulme, *Further Speculations* (Lincoln, 1962), p. 90.

18. J. Hillis Miller, *Poets of Reality*, pp. 309–10.

19. William Carlos Williams, "How To Write," *New Directions in Prose and Poetry*, No. 1 (Norfolk, Conn., 1936), n.p.

20. Ibid.

21. William Carlos Williams, *Briarcliff Quarterly*, III (October 1946), 205, 208.

CHAPTER III

1. For convenience, however, I will make reference to the titles Williams later provided, rather than to the original numbers. The *CEP* has twenty-eight poems in the sequence but its XXVII ("The Hermaphroditic Telephones") was not in the original version.

2. Quoted by Williams in the "Prologue" to *Kora in Hell* (*SE*, p. 12).

3. See Dijkstra, "William Carlos Williams and Painting," pp. 84–89.

4. Quoted by John C. Thirwall, "William Carlos Williams' 'Paterson,' " *New Directions in Prose and Poetry*, No. 17 (Norfolk, Conn., 1961), p. 253.

5. *Leaves of Grass: One Hundred Years After*, ed. Milton Hindus, p. 24.

6. William Carlos Williams, "An Approach to the Poem," pp. 58–59.

CHAPTER IV

1. I am using these writers only to establish a context in which to define and assess Williams. Other critics have suggested direct influence. James Guimond relates *In the American Grain* to Lawrence's *Studies* and the critics connected with the *Seven Arts* magazine in *The Art of William Carlos Williams* (Urbana, Ill., 1968), pp. 65–71; Abraham Dijkstra relates the book to the so-called "American Group" around Alfred Stieglitz in "William Carlos Williams and Painting," pp. 193–225.

2. Waldo Frank, *Our America* (New York, 1919), p. 10.

3. In "William Carlos Williams: On the Road to *Paterson*" and "The Unicorn in *Paterson*: William Carlos Williams"—both collected in *The Poem of the Mind* (New York, 1966), pp. 125–61; Louis Martz uses *In the American Grain* to introduce a discussion of *Paterson;* his student Walter Scott Peterson follows this practice in *An Approach to Paterson* (New Haven, Conn., 1967). Mr. Martz's pieces are important generative studies of Williams, and the Peterson book is an exhaustive study of *Paterson*'s themes, but their format implies a secondary status for *In the American Grain*. In *"In the American Grain:* William Carlos Williams on the Amer-

ican Past," *American Quarterly*, XIX (Fall 1967), 499–515, Alan
Holder argues that Williams's book is "a highly selective, impres-
sionistic account of our history, the product of his imagination
playing over the documents. As might be expected of such a work,
it is not committed to a single, monolithic thesis, but has several
central concerns . . ." (500–1). Mr. Holder thus does not see
either the coherence or the profundity of Williams's book. In the
struggle between will and the land the book does have a unifying
center, and "playing over," as we shall see, is an entirely inaccurate
characterization of Williams's grasp of the documents, which is
often deep and firm. Mr. Holder does attempt to establish Williams's sources, but his study is incomplete—not all available
sources have been cited—and inexact—sometimes wrong transla-
tions are cited.

4. See the discussion in Phillip Damon, "History and Idea in
Renaissance Criticism," in *Literary Criticism and Historical Understanding*, ed. Phillip Damon (New York, 1967), pp. 25–51.

5. The Mather quotations are from *The Wonders of the Invis-
ible World* (London, 1862), pp. 9–14, 129–48, 159–63. Since he
associates the trials with the suppression of natural energy, Williams quotes only accounts of the trials of women, although Mather
also includes the trial of a minister (pp. 149–58).

6. References to Tenochtitlan (*Kora*, p. 40) and Columbus
(*Kora*, p. 34) in *Kora in Hell* indicate that Williams began looking
at these documents as early as 1917, six years before these early
chapters appeared in *Broom*.

7. Alan Holder cites the translation of Rasles's second letter
which appears in Rev. William Ingraham Kip's *The Early Jesuit
Missions in North America* (New York, 1946); but Williams himself cites the original *Lettres Édifiantes* (p. 120), uses both letters
printed there and always quotes the French of the source. Williams
may have discovered Rasles through Kip, but this was one of the
few cases in which he refused to rely on a translation.

8. Sources for the Red Eric chapter are "The Saga of Eric the
Red" and "The Vinland History of the Flat Island Book" in the
translation by Arthur Middleton Reeves. Williams probably found
these documents in *The Northmen, Columbus and Cabot, 985–
1503*, eds. Julius Olson and Edward G. Bourne (New York, 1906),
since this is clearly the book he used for the Columbus chapter.
The first three paragraphs of the Freydis episode are taken from

"The Saga of Eric the Red," pp. 31, 37–38, while the rest is drawn
from "The Vinland History," pp. 62–65. In both cases he sticks
close to the language of the Reeves translation, but he often
edits it in small ways that make the language more economical and
forceful.

9. *Conquest: Dispatches of Cortez from the New World*, eds.
Irwin Blacker and Harry Rosen (New York, 1962), is cited by
Professor Holder. The book reprints a 1906 translation by Francis
A. MacNutt, but Williams used the translation by George Folsom
(New York, 1843), whose wording he often follows very closely
and from whose introduction he has taken the list of artifacts on
pp. 28–29.

10. The main source for the De Soto chapter is the "Relation"
of the journey by the unidentified Hidalgo of Elvas, translated by
Edward G. Bourne in *Narratives of the Career of Hernando
De Soto* (New York, 1904), I, 3–223. Williams also read "Relation"
by De Biedma (ibid. II, 3–40) from which he took a few quotes,
such as "which seemed like a thousand years" (p. 45), "obscure
and intricate parts" (p. 46), and "He went about for the road and
returned to us desperate" (p. 47).

11. A few details—Jefferson's suggestion that Burr get the news
from the papers, Hamilton's confession that he might have been
misinformed of Burr's intentions—are not in Parton and seem to
come from the *Memoirs* (New York, 1837), II, 320, and II, 139,
respectively. But in speaking about Burr's feats in the Revolutionary War, his clash with Washington, his courtship and marriage,
Williams comes close to Parton's wording often enough to show
that he, or his wife, mainly relied on *The Life and Times* (New
York, 1858). The "they say" anecdote with which he concludes
(p. 207) comes directly from Parton, p. 637. It is an index of how
hotheaded Williams's handling of this source was that in the de-
bates over who fired first in the duel with Hamilton, he does not
accept Parton's judicious reconstruction (p. 350), but the one
offered by Burr's seconds, quoted by Parton (p. 617).

12. Benjamin Spencer shows how Williams shifts the meaning
of "local" in order to push his argument; see "Doctor Williams'
American Grain," *Tennessee Studies in Literature*, VIII (1963), 4.

13. Thomas Whitaker, *William Carlos Williams* (New York,
1968), pp. 77–91. I agree with his contention that "in theme and
style, *In the American Grain* is a dialogical encounter with the

New World" (p. 78) but I have extensive disagreement with his application of it.

14. *Broom*, IV (March 1923), 252–60.

15. Williams read the *Journal of the First Voyage*, translated by Sir Clements R. Markham, in *The Northmen, Columbus and Cabot*, eds. Julius Olson and Edward G. Bourne, pp. 89–258. For the fourth voyage he relied on the *Letter of Columbus to the Nurse of Prince John*, translated by George F. Barwick (ibid. pp. 371–83) and the *Letter of Columbus on his Fourth Voyage*, translated by R. H. Major (ibid. pp. 389–418).

16. See, for example, the last four paragraphs of Williams's text (pp. 25–26) which appear to give exact quotation of the *Journal;* but there actually has been a good deal of elision, designed to draw out the basic motive, the true voice, of the young Columbus.

CHAPTER V

1. All of their early critical assessments of Williams have been collected in *William Carlos Williams, A Collection of Critical Essays*, ed. J. Hillis Miller (Englewood Cliffs, N. J., 1966).

2. Thomas Whitaker, *William Carlos Williams*, p. 119.

3. Frank Kermode, *The Sense of an Ending* (New York, 1967), pp. 129–30.

4. *Six American Short Novels*, ed. R. P. Blackmur (New York, 1960).

5. Sherwood Anderson, *Winesburg, Ohio* (New York, 1946), p. 144.

6. Louis Martz, *The Poem of the Mind*, p. 132.

7. William Carlos Williams, " 'White Mule' versus Poetry," *The Writer*, L (August 1937), 243–45.

CHAPTER VI

1. Much more has been written about *Paterson* than Williams's earlier work. Among defenders of the poem are Louis Martz in the two articles already referred to; Sister M. Bernetta Quinn, *The Metamorphic Tradition in Modern Poetry* (New Brunswick, N.J., 1955), pp. 89–129; Walter Sutton, "Dr. Williams' 'Paterson' and the Quest for Form," *Criticism*, II (Summer 1960), 242–59; Roy Harvey Pearce, *The Continuity of American Poetry* (Princeton, N.J.,

1961), pp. 111–30; Walter Scott Peterson, *An Approach to Paterson* (New Haven, Conn., 1967); A. Kingsley Weatherhead, *The Edge of the Image* (Seattle, 1967), pp. 121–36 and *passim;* James Guimond, *The Art of William Carlos Williams*, pp. 153–200; Thomas Whitaker, *William Carlos Williams*, pp. 129–51; Joel Osborne Conarroe, "A Local Pride: The Poetry of *Paterson*," *PMLA*, LXXXIV (May 1969), 547–58.

2. Randall Jarrell, *Poetry and the Age* (New York, 1955), pp. 238–39.

3. Joseph Frank, *The Widening Gyre* (New Brunswick, 1963), p. 19.

4. My discussion of the modern epic here is indebted to Richard Hutson, "The Word Dimensional," unpublished dissertation (University of Illinois, 1967), pp. 33–46.

5. The relationships between Williams and some of his predecessors in the modern long poem is incisively discussed by Joel Conarroe, "A Local Pride: The Poetry of *Paterson*," 548–52.

6. Ibid., 552–58.

7. Ralph Nash, "The Use of Prose in 'Paterson,'" *Perspective*, VI (Autumn–Winter 1953), 194.

8. James Guimond, *The Art of William Carlos Williams*, pp. 175–200.

9. These allusions are discussed most extensively by Walter Scott Peterson, *An Approach to Paterson*, pp. 16, 36n, 62–64, 68–70, 85–86, 95f., 110, 178, 179, 191.

CHAPTER VII

1. This crisis in Williams's career has been examined at length in Sherman Paul's excellent *The Music of Survival* (Urbana, Ill., 1968).

2. Walter Sutton, "Dr. Williams' 'Paterson' and the Quest for Form," 242.

3. Louis Martz, *The Poem of the Mind*, p. 155. Professor Martz himself, however, stresses the "wholeness" of the entire work, Books I–V (p. 156).

4. Quoted in Linda W. Wagner, *The Poems of William Carlos Williams* (Middletown, Conn., 1964), p. 110.

5. For elaboration of this point, see *The Poem of the Mind*, pp. 156f.

6. J. Hillis Miller, *Poets of Reality*, p. 355; Sherman Paul, *The Music of Survival*, p. 1.

7. Because these poems have been more widely accepted, they have been the subject of some perceptive criticism. See *The Music of Survival*, pp. 62–109; *Poets of Reality*, pp. 355–59; A. Kingsley Weatherhead, *The Edge of the Image*, pp. 136–52, 162–69; and Thomas Whitaker, *William Carlos Williams*, pp. 152–63.

Index